Smart Pricing

D1563793

Smart Pricing

How Google, Priceline, and Leading Businesses Use Pricing Innovation for Profitability

Jagmohan Raju
Z. John Zhang

Vice President, Publisher: Tim Moore
Associate Publisher and Director of Marketing: Amy Neidlinger
Editor: Steve Kobrin
Executive Editor: Jeanne Glasser
Editorial Assistant: Myesha Graham
Operations Manager: Gina Kanouse
Senior Marketing Manager: Julie Phifer
Publicity Manager: Laura Czaja
Assistant Marketing Manager: Megan Colvin
Cover Designer: Chuti Prasertsith
Managing Editor: Kristy Hart
Senior Project Editor: Lori Lyons
Copy Editor: Krista Hansing Editorial Services, Inc.
Proofreader: Language Logistics, LLC
Indexer: Erika Millen
Compositor: Nonie Ratcliff
Manufacturing Buyer: Dan Uhrig

© 2015 by Pearson Education, Inc.

Upper Saddle River, New Jersey 07458

For information about buying this title in bulk quantities, or for special sales opportunities (which may include electronic versions; custom cover designs; and content particular to your business, training goals, marketing focus, or branding interests), please contact our corporate sales department at corpsales@pearsoned.com or (800) 382-3419.

For government sales inquiries, please contact governmentsales@pearsoned.com.

For questions about sales outside the U.S., please contact international@pearsoned.com.

Company and product names mentioned herein are the trademarks or registered trademarks of their respective owners.

Printed in the United States of America

3   18

ISBN-10: 0-13-438499-7
ISBN-13: 978-0-13-438499-3

Pearson Education LTD.
Pearson Education Australia PTY, Limited.
Pearson Education Singapore, Pte. Ltd.
Pearson Education North Asia, Ltd.
Pearson Education Canada, Ltd.
Pearson Educación de Mexico, S.A. de C.V.
Pearson Education—Japan
Pearson Education Malaysia, Pte. Ltd.

Library of Congress Cataloging-in-Publication Data is on file.

To our respective families, we dedicate this book.
We understand the price they have paid
for us to write this book.

Contents

Acknowledgments

An old Chinese saying has it that to be a scholar, you must read ten thousand books and travel ten thousand miles. We must have accomplished both a long time ago. However, only in recent years did we realize that we are so indebted to many scholars who had written the ten thousand books that we should repay the debt by contributing one. This urge has grown in recent years as the pricing classes we have taught for more than a decade have grown in popularity. Altogether, we must have taught pricing to four or five thousand people—from undergraduates, MBAs, and EMBAs, to professionals and business executives, both here in the U.S. and in other countries.

Writing this book has been a labor of love for us. In every chapter, we were reminded of all the students we have taught and who taught us. Most of the material contained in this book builds on some of those discussions, which certainly helped to advance our understanding of those issues. For that reason, we want to thank our current and past students at the Wharton School and also at the Olin School of Business, Columbia Business School, UCLA, Indian School of Business (ISB) in India, and at the China-European International Business School (CEIBS) and Cheung Kong graduate School of Business (CKGSB) in China. We hope that they are still passionate about pricing and that they recognize in this book some of the insights they have contributed in class.

Over the years, our primary research interest has been in pricing, and we have collaborated with many first-rate scholars. The contents of this book reflect their influence as well. We want to thank them for working with us and for enriching our knowledge in pricing. They will surely identify their personal and professional influences on us here. For those scholars whose collaborative projects with us were delayed as a result of this book, we also want to thank you for indulging us as we prepared this manuscript. Writing this book turned out to be lot more absorbing and time-consuming than we had anticipated!

We also want to thank our Wharton colleagues for providing an inspiring and caring intellectual environment. With their encouragement, our interest in pricing flourished. Most important, we want to thank Jerry Wind, a prominent marketing scholar and the inaugural editor-in-chief for Prentice Hall, who encouraged us to write this book. Jerry has been a constant source of inspiration and support. He is most generous in offering new ideas to us and most persistent in challenging us to do what he likes to call "impossible thinking." Of course, as much as we try, it is impossible for us to think that this book has met his high expectations.

We also want to thank the editors at Pearson Education, Tim Moore and Jeanne Glasser, for their professional advice and for their patience with us. For the same reason, we are also grateful to Steve Kobrin, the new editor-in-chief for Prentice Hall.

In writing this book, we quickly realized that writing a book for a general business audience is very different from writing academic research papers. For that reason, we are most grateful to Bennett Voyles, who put his professional research and writing expertise at our disposal. Ben is a terrific writer, knowledgeable in many business subjects, and a jolly good fellow to work with. His assistance in writing this book is much appreciated.

Finally, we want to thank our respective families for putting up with us for missing family events, school activities, and weekend games while we worked on the book. We know the price they had to pay for us to complete it. To them, we dedicate this book.

About the Authors

Professor Jagmohan S. Raju is the Joseph J. Aresty Professor at the Wharton School and the Chair of the Marketing Department. He is also the Executive Director of the Wharton-Indian School of Business partnership. Before becoming an academic, Professor Raju worked with the Tata Administrative Service and Philips India Ltd.

He has a Ph.D., M.S., M.A. Stanford University; an MBA from IIM, Ahmedabad; and a BTech from IIT Delhi. He was recognized for the best academic performance in his class for each of the two years he studied at IIM Ahmedabad, a merit scholarship at IIT Delhi, and the President's Gold Medal at Punjab Public School, Nabha.

Professor Raju is the past Marketing Editor of *Management Science* and the Past President of the INFORMS Society for Marketing Science. His main areas of research include competitive marketing strategy, pricing, retailing, sales promotions, sales force compensation, corporate image advertising, and strategic alliances. He has supervised 12 doctoral dissertations to date. He coordinated the Wharton Marketing Department's PhD Program. He serves on Wharton's Academic Personnel Committee, and Globalization Committee.

His research papers have won the John DC Little best paper award (twice), the Frank Bass dissertation paper award (twice) and several other recognitions. He has received several teaching awards, some of which include the George Robbins Teaching Award and Marketing Teacher of the Year while he was at UCLA; Wharton Executive MBA Teaching Awards; Wharton Miller-Sherrerd Core Teaching Award, and the Indian School of Business Teaching Award. Professor Raju teaches the core marketing class and the pricing elective at Wharton.

He lives in Cherry Hill, NJ with his wife Indu, a former banker. Although he is no longer able to play serious sports, he remains an avid fan of cricket, badminton, and field hockey while his colleagues in the department and his three children are helping him learn to appreciate basketball and baseball.

Professor Z. John Zhang is a Professor of Marketing and Murrel J. Ades Professor at The Wharton School of the University of Pennsylvania. He earned a Bachelor's degree in Engineering Automation and Philosophy of Science from Huazhong University of Science and Technology (China), a Ph.D. in History and Sociology of Science from the University of Pennsylvania, and also a Ph.D. in Economics from the University of Michigan.

Prior to joining Wharton in 2002, John taught pricing and marketing management at the Olin School of Business of Washington University in St. Louis for three years and at Columbia Business School for five years. In the past eight years, John has also taught pricing to over two thousand Chinese executives in Mandarin as part of Wharton's executive education and other outreach and collaborative programs. He also won the 2003 EMBA Electives Teaching Award for teaching pricing to Wharton EMBAs.

John's research focuses primarily on competitive pricing strategies, the design of pricing structures, and channel management. He has published many articles in top marketing and management journals on various pricing issues such as measuring consumer reservation prices, price-matching guarantees, couponing, rebates, targeted pricing, access service pricing, choice of price promotion vehicles, channel pricing, price wars, and the pricing implications of combative advertising. In recent years, he has also developed a keen interest in the movie and telecom industries. He has also published a number of articles in Chinese on pricing and retailing issues in China. He currently is collaborating with scholars in many countries to explore various pricing and channel issues in emerging markets and beyond. He won the 2001 John D.C. Little Best Paper Award and the 2001 Frank Bass Best Dissertation Award, along with his co-authors, for his contribution to the understanding of targeted pricing with imperfect targetability.

As part of his service to the marketing community, John serves as Associate Editor for *Quantitative Economics and Marketing*. He is also an area editor for *Marketing Science* and *Management Science*.

John lives in Lower Merion, Pennsylvania, with his wife Lynne and their three children Rae, Neil, and Peter. In his spare time, he likes skiing, rollerblade skating, and going on bike expeditions with Neil and Peter. His favorite pastime: making up pricing puzzles.

Introduction: Fingerprints of the Invisible Hand

After a long season of back-breaking labor seeding, feeding, and growing a crop, a farmer would never say, "Time to harvest—let's take it easy." If anything, the farmer would get up even earlier and go to bed even later to make sure that every last grain was harvested. Yet supposedly sophisticated companies, run by some of the best-educated people in the world, neglect what peasants have known by instinct for thousands of years. They work hard thinking about, growing, and finding markets for their product but then pay scant attention to the decision that determines what all that hard work yields the company: setting the price.

Despite the critical function prices play in corporate profitability, we find that managers with pricing responsibilities do not usually think systematically about their pricing strategies. Most pricing decision makers never look for a strategy that could yield their product's maximum value. According to one study, only a tiny number of firms have "both a pricing strategy and research to support it." When it comes to pricing, some estimated that only about 8% of American businesses can be considered "sophisticated players."[1]

Oddly, nobody seems bothered by this state of affairs. Many executives we talk to about prices say, "We don't set prices. The market does!" As economists, we are not sure what this statement means. "Who is the market, then?" we press them.

To our mind, this is a reasonable question. Price setting is a tangible process with a tangible outcome—a dollar figure. The process of arriving at that number might not be tidy, but it cannot be so mysterious that it does not involve any human intervention. Someone, somewhere must make a concrete, numerical decision about the price of a product or service. Yet managers often give us a bewildered or indignant look when we ask this question and act as if the question itself were frivolous or rude. The way the managers talk about it, setting the price for a product or service is an almost automatic process, outside anyone's control. Occasionally, we get the more profound-sounding answer that "the invisible hand" sets the price—a misapplication of the famous macroeconomic observation of Adam Smith, the great Eighteenth Century Scottish economist and philosopher, on microeconomic circumstance.

Thinking of price-setting as being similar to time or the tide is a comforting idea, given how many company activities require conscious thought. But it's not actually true. When you take a closer look, the hands that set the price are almost always visible. They might not be very nimble, but they can clearly be seen in each of the four most common methods of price setting. Among the least sophisticated companies we have encountered over the years, setting a price sometimes involves not much more work than selecting a lottery number: Pick what comes to mind, say a prayer, and hope for the best. More sophisticated companies don't always do much better. They often take simplistic, ad hoc approaches, such as cost-plus pricing, competition-based pricing, or consumer-based pricing. Each of these approaches requires human intervention, and each is overly simplistic.

Cost-Plus Pricing

An overwhelming majority of U.S. companies use the cost-plus approach to set their prices. This practice also appears to be popular in other markets, even in fast-growing countries such as China and India. To use cost-plus pricing, a firm first determines its sales target and then figures out the average cost it will incur based on the sales target. The price for the product is set by taking the average cost plus a markup. For example, if the sales of Apple's iPod are 2 million units, the average cost at that output level might be $100 per iPod. Assuming that the normal markup at the company is 70%, Apple's selling price for an iPod would be $170. The size of the markup is determined either by the company's targeted internal rate of return on investment or by some vaguely defined "industry convention."

The enduring appeal of the cost-plus approach is threefold. First, it is simple. The manager does not need to look outside the company's own ledger to determine the price for a product. A casual familiarity with arithmetic is sufficient for anyone to come up with a price. Second, it is fair, or appears so. Indeed, cost-plus pricing is said to date back to medieval times when churches were involved in regulating commerce and allowed merchants to make only a fair living, not a killing. Third, many practitioners will tell you that cost-plus pricing is financially prudent because it ensures profitable sales. This guarantee of prudence is a reassuring way to dodge the high pressure involved in making a pricing decision. Such pressure can be nerve-racking at times because the effects of a pricing decision, unlike many other decisions in a corporation, are typically immediate and conspicuous.

However, none of these three reasons is sufficient justification for adopting a conventional cost-plus strategy. First, why is simple better? A quick counterexample suggests otherwise. When a consumer in China purchases a beautiful silk scarf, does she know or care about the cost of making the scarf? Most likely, she does not. In fact, manufacturers themselves might not even know the costs of their products with any degree of precision. In that case, why should a silk manufacturer set its price solely based on its costs?

A Chinese silk manufacturer we know tried this simple approach. The company set a low price of 200–300 yuan for its scarves. Its cost of production was so low that even 200 yuan would still yield a decent margin. This low price was also extremely competitive, compared to the high price of 2,000–3,000 yuan set by a French company in China selling similar scarves sourced—you guessed it—from this very manufacturer. On paper, the Chinese company looked as if it should be very competitive in the marketplace, given its huge price advantage. Yet somehow the French company still outsold the Chinese manufacturer by a big margin, even with an identical product that cost ten times as much.

The difference was so great that branding alone could not explain the outcome, a fact that baffled company strategists. Later, it dawned on the executives that the low price itself might be the problem. Most of the manufacturer's customers purchased a silk scarf not for their own use, but as an elegant gift to the wives of their bosses or *guanxi* (connections). Potential customers looked at the 200–300 yuan price tag and decided it was simply not substantial enough to be the kind of door-opening gift they had in mind. Many forgone sales later, the manufacturer learned to look beyond its cost and set its prices based on a better understanding of its customers and the market.

The second advantage touted for cost-plus pricing is its supposed fairness. But we think this often is not true, either. For example, if a utility company is regulated such that it can charge a rate based only on its average cost plus a fair return on investment, many economic studies have shown that the utility company will have little incentive to minimize its costs, and the rate will drift up unnecessarily in the long run. For the same reason, if other kinds of firms always succeed in passing their costs on to consumers in this way, they have no incentive to minimize their costs. Finally, if the cost of serving customers is the same, is it fair to charge all customers the same price, even if they have varying incomes and need for the product? Perhaps the answer will vary, depending on your political convictions and economic circumstances, but a little thinking makes it clear that in many situations "fair" cost-plus accounting could lead to an unfair result.

Consider an example from the pharmaceutical industry. If a drug is cheap to develop and manufacture, should it always be sold cheaply? Is a 10% markup on some cheap ingredients really a fair return on intellectual property that reduced doctor visits, hospital stays, and employee absenteeism for thousands of people?

Perhaps it would be more fair for society to reward the innovator. It might even be socially beneficial in the long run to allow a higher price as an incentive to encourage others to try to solve similar problems.

Consumers, interestingly, have a surprisingly nuanced view of fairness in cost-plus pricing. If cost-plus pricing is a fair way to set the price, then if a firm's unit cost decreases by $10, the absolutely fair thing to do would be to lower the product's price by $10 plus the markup on the cost. However, studies have shown that the fairness standard people apply to price changes is far more favorable to a firm than the cost-plus pricing rule would suggest, even when they know the precise magnitude of the cost change. In one survey, half of the respondents agreed with the statement that "fairness does not require the firm to pass on any part of its savings."[2] However, in that same survey, consumers also believed that more cost savings should be passed on to consumers if the cost savings are the result of a reduction of input costs instead of an efficiency gain: If the price of jet fuel goes down, I want a discount on my ticket, but if you build a better airplane, you can keep the difference. By applying this fixed cost-plus rule, a firm forgoes its chance of achieving any gains from efficiency improvements, although its customers would not have minded.

Nor does cost plus-pricing mean that every sale is automatically profitable. Cost is often partly a function of the sales target. If sales fall short of the target, the actual cost might be higher than projected. In that case, the price could turn out to be too low. Such a shortfall is always possible because the people responsible for sales normally make the sales projection, and they have an intrinsic interest in engineering a lower price to boost sales or to make their selling job easier.

Even if the sales target is met or exceeded, we don't know whether the initial price is a good price or one that a company can improve for its own financial benefit. Regardless of actual sales, cost-plus pricing does not ensure or even encourage financial prudence.

Finally, as the Chinese scarf example suggests, the biggest problem with cost-plus pricing is that it is an inward-looking approach that tends to distract a company from its customer orientation and obscure the importance of detailed market research. A corporation that develops an entrenched culture in price setting based on cost-plus pricing encourages *ad hoc* pricing decisions and overlooks many opportunities for price improvements. Indeed, cost-plus pricing sometimes leads companies to set consistently sub-par prices. When sales are brisk, a company will lower its price as its average costs go down, but when sales are sluggish, it raises its price to "cover" its higher average cost.

Competition-Based Pricing

Competition-based pricing is the second-most-popular price-setting approach. Managers sometimes refer to this approach as strategic pricing, although it's not particularly strategic. When taking this approach, a firm simply checks out its competition's price and then sets the price of its own product at about the same level, plus or minus a few percent. Once again, this approach has the virtue of being simple: It's an easy way to make a pricing decision without having to conduct any thorough market research. It also seems relatively safe: By setting a price close to the rival's and adjusting with it, a firm does not risk losing its market share to the competition.

However, setting one's own price solely on the basis of competition's price can cause two problems, either of which can cost a company dearly.

The worst risk is that competition-based pricing lulls the price setter into passivity. Managers can be so taken by this pricing approach that they lose sight of their own pricing responsibilities. To them, pricing involves nothing more than monitoring competitors' prices and making some timely adjustments on their own price based on the competition's price. Maybe this is what managers mean when they say the invisible hand sets their prices. This might seem like a low-risk strategy, but unfortunately sometimes the competition decides to set its prices the same way. When this kind of double-mirroring occurs, prices not just for the company but for the entire industry can easily fall out of sync with current demand.

Other times, price-matching can lead to a game of chicken. Everyone knows that setting a low price is the easiest, fastest way to gain market share. The trouble is that one rarely encounters a company that does not want a larger market share: In any given industry, if you added up all the market share targets of each company, the sum would most likely far exceed 100%. Obviously, something has to give. If all the firms in an industry become overzealous about meeting their market share targets, prices can easily slip into a downward spiral that can hurt not just the company but the industry as a whole. The competition for market share between the two aerospace giants Boeing and Airbus in the mid- and late 1990s offers an example of this risk. At the time, Airbus was consistently gaining market share and had surpassed its self-determined "survival threshold" of 30% of new global commercial airplane orders. Boeing decided to respond. It would "beat back Airbus and retain supremacy in the commercial-jetliner industry,"[3] and fearlessly guard its 60% market share. Boeing and Airbus began competing vigorously, "making every bid a battle-ground." Each would slash its price by at least 20% off the list price to grab an order. For example, to bid for ValueJet's order of 50 100-passenger airplanes in 1995, Boeing reportedly brought its price for Boeing 737s down from the list of $35 million, below its rock-bottom price of $22 million, all the way to $19 million.[4]

The outcome was quite predictable: huge losses all around. Boeing temporarily won the share battle for new airplane orders.

However, the victory came at a horrendous cost. Boeing suffered its first annual loss in 50 years in 1997, and by the following year, the company was forced to take more than $3 billion of pretax charges for the foul-up. Between 1996 and 1998, the profit margin of Boeing's commercial jetliners fell from 10% to less than 1%—a lower margin than a corner grocery store.

We are not suggesting that firms should never compete on price to gain market share. As we show in Chapter 3, "The Art of Price Wars," price wars are a legitimate strategy. However, we are suggesting—and advocating throughout this book—that firms should learn how to compete as intelligently on price as they do on every other aspect of their business. Adam Smith's invisible hand works only if the economic agents in the market are driven by their own enlightened self-interest to pursue their own maximum economic gain. Boeing's decision to build extraordinarily complex aerospace vehicles at a lower margin than a corner grocer was not enlightened self-interest.

Consumer-Based Pricing

Consumer-based pricing is the third common approach firms use to set their prices. In this case, the firm first sizes up its customers to determine how much each customer is willing to pay for its product or service and then charges the price each customer is willing to bear. Car dealers often take this approach.[5] A dealer typically displays a high sticker price for a car, which is nothing more than a wished-for price intended to frame the value of the car for the customer. Then a salesperson takes the prospective buyer out for a test drive. In the process, the salesperson gathers information about the customer's job, hobbies, family, and so on to help size up how serious the shopper is about the car and how price-sensitive he might be. When the salesperson senses that price is not a primary concern or that the customer is not a deft haggler, he will typically give all kinds of reasons for not being able to bring down the list price much. However, if the salesperson senses that the price is the obstacle to closing the deal, the salesperson will offer a better discount—but only after securing the "reluctant" approval of a mysterious boss behind a closed door and shaded windows.

Customer-based pricing gives the company the flexibility to charge different prices to different customers, rising or falling to match the size of the customer's wallet. Theoretically, the firm can achieve a high volume of sales at the best possible margins. However, an obvious problem with this pricing approach is that it inevitably alienates those customers who end up paying more than the successful hagglers. In the case of car purchases, many economic studies have shown that minority men and women have to pay up to $1,060 more than white males for the same car.[6] The backlash against this discriminatory practice contributed to the enormous success of GM's no-hassle, no-haggle sales policy on its Saturn line in the 1990s.

In business-to-business markets, discriminatory pricing can also easily alienate a firm's best customers, with detrimental long-term consequences. The worst is that over time, discriminatory pricing can train the customers to become aggressive bargainers. In the industrial markets, a professional buyer fears a high relative price more than a high price. A high price is a problem for the industry. A high relative price is a problem for the buyer personally. No one wants to think of himself as a sucker, but for a professional buyer, the damage wrought by overpaying isn't only to his pride; it can also hurt his career. He may suffer professionally if he is exposed as less skillful than his peers. Consequently, if the buyer suspects price discrimination, he will do everything possible to exploit a seller's pricing flexibility to secure the lowest price.

Ultimately, this kind of strategy can train good customers to behave badly. If a buyer knows the price she will pay depends on her perceived willingness to pay, she certainly does not have any incentive to dwell on how good and how valuable the seller's products and services are. Nor can she afford to appear interested in the seller's value propositions. The potential buyer might also try to withhold useful information from the seller, just to conceal her hand. She might even take pains to act as if the seller's products and services are no better, if not worse, than anyone else's—a hint that the buyer is perfectly willing to walk away if the seller's price is not competitive. Frequently, the concealment comes at the cost of depriving the seller of the kind of information that would help the seller serve the buyer better, both now and in the future.

This behavior also encourages more comparison shopping. To ensure a rock-bottom deal, the buyer will look to gain an upper hand in sales negotiations by entertaining competitive offers, even if the buyer does not intend to switch suppliers. Collecting competitive bids gives the buyer a decisive advantage. A seller risks legal perils if he talks to other suppliers about pricing, but a buyer is free to solicit competing price quotes. The buyer can then use the quotes as a lever to gain concessions from the seller. Knowing that the seller's salespeople have some pricing discretion, the buyer will try every means, both carrots and sticks, to make sure that the seller doesn't hold anything back.

For example, it is not uncommon for the buyer to embellish price quotes a little to gain a larger price concession. Sometimes those quotes don't even need to be explicit. A former Merrill Lynch chief information officer is famed for having a million-dollar coffee mug: "When an IBM salesman came calling, the CIO would put a coffee mug from a competitor on his desk. The salesman would immediately cut $1 million off the price of each mainframe, for fear of having Merrill take its huge business elsewhere."[7]

This kind of aggressive negotiation leads both buyer and seller to focus on transactions instead of building a relationship and to channel creative energy into devising ways to win more or less money instead of forging a long-term, win-win partnership. Facing such a buyer, the seller's choice is limited, especially in a buyer's market. You can refuse to budge on the buyer's price demand and try to sell based on a value proposition. In that case, you risk losing a big customer. Or you can compromise, bring the price down promptly, and close the deal. For most commissioned salespeople, such as the IBM salesman facing Merrill's mug of doom, a lower margin is always more appealing than no deal.

The game leaves both sides less happy than they might be. The buyer won't be happy, even if she receives the full discount for which she asked, simply because she can never be certain about whether she could have won an even lower price—so the next time, she will ask for a little more. For the seller, every order costs a little more price integrity. Sometimes this reluctant price discounting can even evolve into an arms race between competitors. Buyers become more demanding, and salespeople ask for more pricing discretion. The salespeople have a good chance of getting such price cuts because they supposedly know customers and competitive situations in the market-place firsthand. And when they have the price cuts, they will use them more freely, forcing the producer to cut costs.

In this kind of pricing environment, the seller has little incentive to invest in the customer relationship or additional services, and cost cutting becomes the paramount imperative. What typically follows can be best described as a kind of service version of Gresham's law: Bad service companies drive out good. If no buyer seems to care about or wants to pay for customer services, then no seller wants to spend money to provide them. As customer service deteriorates in an industry, product differentiation declines, a new round of downward pricing pressure gains momentum, and the product moves another step closer toward being a commodity. Put it all together, and the industry enters a downward spiral, with the buyers paying less and getting less, and the sellers getting less and giving less. It's a good topic to reflect on during your next long-distance flight—over your lunch of peanuts and soda pop.

From this brief tour of how firms set their prices, we can come to two conclusions. First, the market does not set prices. Marketers do. All the prices we observe in the marketplace do not just spring out of an autonomous, impersonal market. The managers' hands in setting those prices are entirely "visible," regardless of whether such interventions are acts of expediency or strategy. Second, cost-plus pricing, competition-based pricing, consumer-based pricing, and even "lottery" pricing are not necessarily the best ways to price a product or service. In many cases, they are nothing but shortcuts managers use to cope with the weight of their decision-making responsibility.

Unfortunately, ignorance of the power of pricing can have huge consequences. Your company's survival may even depend on your pricing strategies. If you are a retailer, you must pay attention to Wal-Mart's price-dominance strategy. Either find a way to cope with it or be steamrolled, as many have been. If you are a manufacturer in the United States, whether you are in textiles, steel, or consumer electronics, you must heed "the China price"—the price quotes from China that are typically 30–50% lower than state-side manufacturing.[8] If you are a financial service company, you must navigate the new reality of deregulations and discount brokerage, both online and offline. Even if you are a high-tech company, you might find yourself in a situation where you no longer enjoy a comfortable lead in technology and you must compete directly or indirectly with companies from South Korea, Taiwan, India, and China—almost always on price and always against a player with a lower cost structure.

Competitors are not the only risk for sellers. Buyers are not as docile as they once were, either. In the consumer market, the Internet has changed the way in which price information is disseminated in the marketplace. A consumer shopping for a car is no longer in the dark about prices. She can easily find information online about the prices different dealers charge for the same car. If she is diligent, she can even find a dealer's invoice price for a car and the amount of the manufacturer's ongoing coupon or rebate promotions on the car. Armed with the price information, the customer might travel hundreds of miles for a lower price and save hundreds or even thousands of dollars on a car purchase. In the industrial market, the Internet plays a simi-lar role in increasing price transparency and expanding the geograph-ical range in which a firm can source its suppliers. As a buyer, when you have extensive price information and a larger set of choices, you become more sophisticated in using that information and choosier in your buying decisions. When you have those savvy buyers in a market, the overall price becomes even more critical for the company.

Price is also becoming more important because product differen-tiation is harder to achieve in many industries. For example, most desktop or laptop computers have "Intel Inside" and run Microsoft Windows. In the service industries, which now account for more than two-thirds of U.S. gross domestic product (GDP), companies cannot patent their service designs in the same way manufacturers patent their product designs. The resulting lack of product differentiation, either real or perceived, and the new ease of comparison shopping inevitably make price a bigger factor in customer buying decisions.

But at the same time technology is changing cost structures and pricing pressures, it is also giving many companies a whole new set of pricing opportunities. Many industries now have a high fixed cost, typically in development, and a low variable cost in production. In the software industry, for example, a huge cost must be incurred up front to develop the first copy of a program, but the cost of replicating the software is nearly zero. The same is true for many other digital tech-nology–based industries such as music, movies, and information, and, to a lesser extent, for service industries such as airlines and hotels.

In these kinds of industries, pricing can play a considerable role because of a low variable cost and a wide dispersion in the con-sumer's willingness to pay. Companies with this kind of cost structure can set prices in ways that either harm profitability or enhance it. An undisciplined manager might seek a quick "high" in volume through an unsustainably low price. On the other hand, a more sophisticated manager might take advantage of the situation by designing a creative pricing structure to attract a certain kind of profitable cus-tomer. In either case, the price is now becoming an increasingly important differentiator.

The Four Levers

A manager can pull only four levers to increase a firm's profitabil-ity: sales, variable costs, fixed costs, and price. When a manager bumps up his firm's advertising budget to gain a larger market share, he's pulling the sales lever. If he has found a cheaper way to source raw materials, he is pulling a variable cost lever. If he tries to reduce his firm's overhead, he is pulling the fixed cost lever. Yet for some rea-son, not all these levers are treated equally. Price, in particular, is neg-lected. This is peculiar because a number of studies have found that although rarely pulled, the price lever is the most efficient way to increase a firm's profitability.[9] We updated these studies by applying the same methodology to the most recent company data available through Wharton Research Data Services (WRDS), as shown in Figure I.1.

As Figure I.1 shows, our analysis essentially reconfirms previous studies. We find that if a firm can cut its fixed costs by 1% without affecting its operations, its profitability can increase, on average, by 2.45%. Similarly, if a firm can increase its sales by 1% without chang-ing its cost structure or price, the firm's profitability can rise by 3.28%. The effect of lowering the variable cost by 1% is larger: Profitability can increase 6.52%. However, the effect of improving a firm's price by 1% is the largest of all: 10.29%. Remarkably, as Figure I.2 shows, this effectiveness ranking order holds for each of the eight industry groups using the standard industry classification (SIC) scheme.

A pessimist might conclude from these numbers that price isn't a lever that one should pull lightly: If the upside benefit of pulling that lever is high, the downside risk or the difficulty involved in pulling that lever must be substantial, too. Otherwise, why wouldn't firms pull that lever more often? Indeed, some managers would quickly add that it's not practical. "It is one thing to cut costs by 1% without affecting everything else, but it is entirely something else to improve your pricing by 1% without changing anything else. For one thing, sales will drop!" For that reason, the pessimist might see the promised double-digit increase in profits as a dangerous illusion. It might seem far more prudent to pull the other three levers instead of risking everything on a single number.

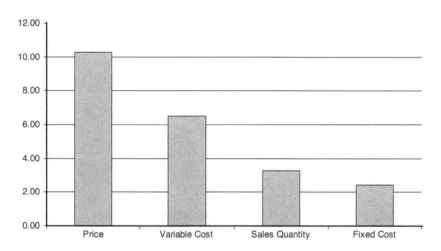

Figure I.1   Impact of profit levers in U.S. in 2004

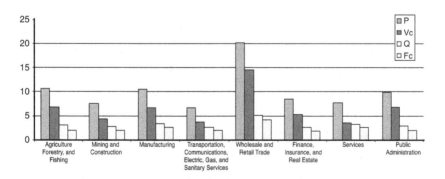

Figure I.2   Impact of profit levers in U S. by industry (2004)

However, an optimist would see from these tantalizing numbers a holy grail for profitability. How often could one identify and work with something that can lead to a double-digit increase in a firm's profitability by just changing a few numbers? The fact that a firm is not pulling the price lever only means that it is missing a big opportunity. After years of diminishing returns with the other three levers, the price lever might just be the best bet. In any case, it's certainly the easiest: Companies can make price changes quickly—hashed out over a bottle of Bud, then approved at the stroke of a pen.

When it comes to the potential of pricing, both the optimist and the pessimist have valid points. However, we believe the optimists have the edge. No strategy is risk-free, but after years of teaching pricing to our MBA students and executives and consulting to pricing managers all over the world, we believe companies willing to pull the price lever face more promise than risk.

Conclusion

Farmers do not take it easy at harvest time. Nor should firms. In our mind, it is simply an untenable management strategy to focus on value creation without thinking about how that value will be captured. The sooner firms recognize this, the sooner they will be on their way to bringing in a bumper crop.

We're not saying that pulling the price lever is a cinch. You must know what you are doing before you even think about pulling that lever. Once pulled, everything can change. Profits either rise spectacularly or fall in a traumatic, humiliating way. Whether you succeed or fail, the effect of your "hand" will be very "visible." Clearly, pricing is not a game for the fainthearted or someone with a trembling hand. But that doesn't mean you should not try. Risks and difficulty are inherent in any important corporate decision. They have not stopped managers from making those decisions and pulling the costs and sales levers in the past. They should not stop managers from facing up to their responsibility to examine the price lever now.

However, pricing is an unfamiliar subject for most managers. Until recently, pricing was scarcely taught except as a unit of microeconomics and a subtopic of marketing. For the longest time, business education everywhere focused primarily on the other three profit levers. Business students learned that in a competitive market, prices should be set so that marginal revenue matches marginal costs. They also learned that competing on price is generally a last resort and probably a bad idea. Unfortunately, neither precept offers much guidance to pricing managers. For these managers, they need more actionable pricing knowledge.

Over the past decade, nearly a dozen books have been published on pricing to help disseminate that knowledge, but most are quite specific, lacking general interests. In this book, we aim to make pricing knowledge more tangible, concrete, and fun by showing how innovative pricing strategies have helped leading companies create and capture value as well as new customers. We visit restaurants where the customer sets the price and see a famous rock band that made money by giving away its album for free. We look at how Google and other high-tech companies have used pricing to remake whole industries, and at China, where executives have made an art out of initiating and fighting price wars—in spite of the conventional Western wisdom that price wars are risky, stupid, and sometimes even fatal.

From these stories and many others, you will see that companies price their products in many different ways—through high prices, low prices, even no price—and you will learn how, why, and when each method works. We hope that as you read these stories, you will learn something not just about how to set prices, but about the importance of thinking about prices. We believe you will agree with us that the possibilities of pricing are endless, limited only by the need to retain some value for future harvest and the bounds of creativity.

Our experience has taught us that pulling the price lever demands courage and confidence, the kind best built on your knowledge about what pricing can do, how you can price your goods or services, and how consumers and your competition might react to your pricing decisions. If this book helps you gain more confidence in pulling the price lever and perhaps sparks an idea about an innovative way to price your own product or service, we will have achieved our main objective.

Endnotes

[1]Kevin J. Clancy and Robert S. Shulman, *The Marketing Revolution*, HarperBusiness, 1991, 144–145.

[2]Daniel Kahneman, Jack L. Knetsch, and Richard H. Thaler, "Fairness and the Assumptions of Economics," *Journal of Business* 59, no. 4 (1986): 285–300.

[3]Frederic M. Biddle and John Helyar, "Flying Low—Behind Boeing's Woes: Clunky Assembly Line, Price War with Airbus—Fearing Loss of Market Share, Company Took Orders It Wasn't Equipped to Fill—Those 737s in the Shadows," *The Wall Street Journal* (April 24, 1998), A1.

[4]Howard Banks, "Profitless Prosperity," *Forbes* 156, no. 11 (November 6, 1995): 64–65.

[5]Preyas S. Desai and Devavrat Purohit, "Let Me Talk to My Manager: Haggling in a Competitive Environment," *Marketing Science*, Spring 2004; 23: 219–233.

[6]John Yinger, "Evidence on Discrimination in Consumer Markets," *The Journal of Economic Perspectives* 12, no. 2 (Spring, 1998): 23–40.

[7]Justin Martin, "Bull Headed," *Context Magazine* (September/October 1999): http://www.contextmag.com/setSearch.asp.

[8]Pete Engardio and Dexter Roberts, "The China Price," *BusinessWeek* (December 6, 2004): 102.

[9]Michael V. Marn and Robert L. Rosiello, "Managing Price, Gaining Profit," *Harvard Business Review* (September 1996): 84–95.

1

"Pay As You Wish" Pricing

"If it's good enough, people will put a penny in the pot."
Chris Hufford, manager, Radiohead

On October 9, 2007, the English alternative rock band Radiohead began an experiment: Instead of pricing its music the conventional way, the band would let its fans pay whatever they wanted to download its latest 10-song album, *In Rainbows*. At the checkout page of the inrainbows.com website, visitors came to an empty price box. When they clicked on the box, a message appeared that said, "It's up to you." On the next page, another message appeared that said, "No, really, it's up to you."

Radiohead's decision to leave pricing to its fans came after years of frustration with traditional distribution. The Oxfordshire-bred band had decided not to renew its contract with its old record label, EMI, after their agreement ended in 2003. Although the five-member band had sold more than 20 million records through conventional channels, with more music being swapped or downloaded in pirated versions on the Internet, the idea of working with a traditional record label that sold albums for a fixed price "felt like chaining ourselves to a dinosaur," says Colin Greenwood, the band's bass player.[1]

Then manager Chris Hufford had an idea: Let the fans pay whatever they wanted for a download. "We all thought he was barmy," confessed singer Thom Yorke. "As we were putting up the site, we were still saying, 'Are you sure about this?'"[2]

Radiohead's pricing strategy set off a fierce debate in the music business, "as though a grenade had been lobbed into a record industry already in disarray," as one music writer put it.[3] On one side stood those who saw the technique as an important experiment in an industry profoundly shaken by the shift from physical to virtual delivery. On the other side, traditionalists who saw "pay as you wish," or what the English call "honor box" payment, as capitulation to the pirates—the beginning of another chapter in the decline and fall of the music business.

By the time the program ended on October 29, 2007, Radiohead had clearly won its bet that "virtual busking," as Hufford called it, could beat conventional pricing and distribution.[4] More than 1.8 million people downloaded the album, and although 60% did not pay, 40% did, which was enough to make the album a success for Radiohead.

Radiohead customers paid $2.26 per album on average, probably generating more cash for the band than if it had sold the album through layers of middlemen using conventional pricing, according to a survey by Comscore, a U.S. e-commerce survey company. (The band's managers disavowed Comscore's estimate but declined to supply an alternative set of numbers.)[5] "In terms of digital income, we've made more money out of this record than out of all the other Radiohead albums put together, forever," says Radiohead singer Thom Yorke.[6]

Some fans claimed to have paid even more than they would have for a conventional album: $20–$30 or more—money they would not have paid under a conventional pricing scheme. Consider Jason Raney of Sacramento, California, who said he planned to pay "a hundred dollars American" for his download of In Rainbows.[7]

Why Pay More?

At first glance, "pay as you wish" pricing doesn't seem to make much sense: Why would anyone pay something for a product if they had the choice to pay nothing? To anyone used to modern shopping, where most products are sold at a set price, "pay as you wish" seems like a utopian rocker's fantasy ("Dude, let's just, like, *ask* them to pay what they want.")—a good idea for a song, maybe, but not necessarily for a purchasing system.

In certain circumstances, however, "pay as you wish" can be very successful. For decades, theaters in the United States and England have offered "pay what you can" performances on certain nights. Several restaurants and cafés across the United States operate on a similar self-determined pricing model in which customers determine the prices. One World Café in Salt Lake City, Utah, is one such restaurant. As *TIME* wrote, "Attorneys and CEOs, students, seniors, and soccer moms, as well as those down on their luck are among the 150–200 customers that dine daily at One World."[8] Although no customer is required to pay, One World Café is still a thriving business. *The Wall Street Journal* reported that the business has been profitable since 2005 and projects revenues of $350,000 this year, with about a 5% profit margin,[9] not out of line with the 4%–6% profit margins typical of small restaurants.[10]

"Pay as you wish" is less impractical than it sounds because it eliminates many of the disadvantages of set pricing. For the seller, a set price requires figuring out what the price should be, which is typically a difficult and time-consuming process: What is this product worth to my customers? What price will enable me to make the most profit, given the fact that, except for certain kinds of luxury goods, a trade-off always occurs between price and volume? The trade-off arises because set pricing typically charges everyone the same price, regardless of whether one is willing to pay more or less. As a result, the seller is always torn between a better margin and a higher volume, as a better margin always results in a lower volume. The only latitude is the capability to adjust the set price over time. However, even with that little latitude, the vexing question for the seller is always "When should I raise or lower my price next?" The costs associated with this kind of activity aren't insignificant. As much as 1.93% of GDP is eaten up setting and resetting retail prices, an activity that economists call the "menu cost."[11]

For buyers, set pricing also requires answering some difficult questions: How much is this product really worth? Is the price I see on the box the right price for this product? This can be especially tricky when the product is something consumers could never manufacture for themselves, such as a digital camera. Even if buyers have all those questions figured out, they might still wonder if they could get a better price somewhere else.

Set pricing makes every transaction an adversarial encounter, a conflict in which neither the seller nor the buyer ever leaves completely satisfied. The seller must be forever uncertain about whether he set the price too low and left money on the table or whether he set the price too high and lost some potentially profitable customers. At the same time, the buyer will never be absolutely sure the deal he received is the best possible deal he might have found if he had kept shopping.

"Pay as you wish" sidesteps all these issues. In a way, it's the fulfillment of a marketer's dream: The seller gets the best offer from every possible buyer, with no chance that the buyer will leave feeling that he overpaid. Instead of choosing a single price that will be either lower or higher than the potential customer is willing to pay, "pay as you wish," creates a market in which the seller can sell to every possible customer at exactly the price the customer is willing to pay, theoretically expanding the market to the broadest possible size without giving too much of a break to those who are happy to pay a higher price.

Although "pay as you wish" pricing has always existed on the margins of the service economy—think of bellhops or street performers—awareness of its possibilities now seems to be spreading. The rise of more products that are entirely intellectual property with very little physical cost, such as software, and the growth of the service economy are making "pay as you wish" an increasingly practical alternative.

It's even making some inroads into academia. One Columbia Business School marketing professor recently experimented with "pay as you wish" pricing for his new textbook.

Noel Capon likens the textbook industry to the cartel price structure U.S. airlines enjoyed in the 1960s, in which the airlines competed on service but never on price. A "cozy oligopoly" of publishers he says, keeps prices high and encourages the publishers to compete for authors and compete over quality but never price. Incensed by the high price of college textbooks, Capon decided that instead of working with a conventional publisher, he would allow students free online access to his new tome.[12]

By copying the Radiohead model for his new marketing book, Capon hopes to force traditional publishers to lower the prices of their textbooks, playing a role analogous to the one low-cost Southwest Airlines played in revolutionizing airline pricing.

The marketing professor also hopes that the ability to read the book with no obligation to buy will prove a good way to boost demand. "It's a way of getting my book into the hands of as many people as possible," he explains. "The major barrier I've had to overcome is the reluctance of instructors to switch books. By taking the price of the online version to zero, instructors who weren't interested at the old price are going to have to give my book a serious thought."[13] (One problem with the theory, however, is that Professor Capon is assuming that instructors care about the price students pay for a textbook—a questionable assertion.

This might not always be the case, in the same way doctors might not care about the price patients pay for prescription drugs.)

For Radiohead, "pay as you wish" had a number of special advantages, too, some unique to the music industry. First, Radiohead's decision to let the public set the price of its product was big news, not only to Radiohead fans, but also to the general public. Choosing this innovative pricing model generated a lot of free publicity, which enabled the band to cut through the clutter of all bands trying to sell music the conventional way.

The notoriety seems to have helped generate a high enough profile for the album that, despite 1.8 million downloads, the "free" album still succeeded as a teaser for a deluxe boxed set (which included a bonus disc with eight additional songs) priced at £40. The boxed set soared to the top of British pop charts on release in December 2007 and sold 95,000 copies by March 2008.[14] In the end, a year after the experiment, Warner/Chappell, Radiohead's publisher, said that the group earned more money on the online downloads of *In Rainbows* than it had from the total sales of its previous album, *Hail to the Thief*. All told, 3 million copies of *In Rainbows* were downloaded or sold. Nor do physical sales seem to have been cannibalized: As of October 2008, a year after the release, CD sales had reached 1.75 million, a few thousand less than the total cumulative sales of its 2001 and 2003 albums combined.[15]

Interestingly, Capon's textbook sale also sought to capture different ends of the demand curve by differentiating the product itself. He offered "pay as you wish" access for a copy, but readers could access it only online. Students whose budget permitted could buy a printed version for $45 or download a portable document format (PDF) for $25.

This capability to structure multiple tiers of demand for the same product is an important feature of many "pay as you wish" programs. Charities and nonprofit groups have long known the advantages of "pay as you wish" pricing: Many of the 5 million visitors a year to the Metropolitan Museum of Art in New York pay $20 a person to enter, despite a sign that clearly specifies that the price is a "suggested donation." Even political marketers have learned the advantages of "pay as you wish": They can make a good case that President Obama's biggest fund-raising innovation wasn't the use of the Internet as a sales channel, but the ability to reach hundreds of thousands of small donors with a "pay as you wish" proposition in a market that, until recently, targeted only institutions and wealthy individuals.

Don't underestimate the value of such exposure in cross-selling. For many bands, recorded music is becoming more important as a way to drive ticket sales for concert tours than a revenue stream in its own right. The reason selling thousands of tickets is better than selling millions of albums right now is because the top performer typically receives up to 90% of the ticket price, as opposed to a much lower share of the price of an album.[16] For example, pop star Justin Timberlake earned $70.6 million on a 2007 tour in North America, even as his albums earned only $20.8 million.[17]

This isn't an isolated case. "Artists have found that their prime income stream is coming from touring," says one music industry analyst. "Twenty years ago, artists toured to promote an album. Today artists tour because there is a demand to see them live and that's how they make their money."[18] One measure of the success of touring today is that some music labels are reportedly trying to sign artists to "360" contracts, which give the company a share not just of the music revenue, but also of the revenue from T-shirts, concert tickets, ring tones, and other products related to the music.

Looked at in this light, even giving the music away can be a winning strategy. For example, Prince did not earn a profit on the nearly three million *Planet Earth* CDs sent out with the London *Daily Mail* newspaper this spring, but partly on the strength of that promotion, he was able to sell out 21 London concerts.[19] His "loss" with the album clearly sparked interest in his live performances, likely earning him more than the reported $500,000 plus 10% royalty he would have made on the sale of each CD distributed by conventional means.[20]

Many people, particularly college students, already pay nothing for their music and grow their music collection by downloading pirated versions. Instead of extracting nothing, as often happens in the current system of music distribution, Radiohead probably converted some of those online freeloaders to paying customers: A quarter might not be much, but it's better than nothing.

Although media would seem like a very special case, other kinds of businesses—even restaurants, as mentioned earlier—have also adopted "pay what you wish" pricing. Terra Bite Lounge, a coffee shop located in Kirkland, a suburb of Seattle, Washington, is one case in which the benefits of this alternative pricing method are not clearcut. The café does not list its prices. Customers pay whatever they wish and drop their payments in a locked metal box on the counter, discreetly labeled "All payments and tips here, please." According to *The Wall Street Journal*, Terra Bite serves an average of 200 customers per day, who each pay on average $2 to $3. Ervin Peretz, one of the owners, says Terra Bite's per-food item revenue is substantially less than other coffee shops. At the moment, Terra Bite is a financially viable business and has more than broke even operationally since it opened in November 2007, but its unique pricing policy might put it in a precarious situation.[21] Serving an average of 80 customers per day at $3 per transaction is barely the break-even point, especially considering its rent of $4,000 per month.[22] However, others have done much better. At one café in Kettering, Ohio, the owner switched to "pay as you wish" pricing in 2008 as a way to respond to the recession. The result: Since he switched to that pricing method, sales and customer head count are up 50%–100%, and he's thinking of adding more staff.[23] And he's not alone: The upscale Just Around the Corner restaurant in London is now in its twenty-second year of operation using "pay as you wish" pricing, and it's still apparently successful.

So why take the risk? "When you give people good food and good service, they leave bigger tips," explains Vasos Michael, owner of Just Around the Corner. "So I said to myself, 'Let's leave the bill up to them, too.'"[24]

Typically, sellers turn to "pay as you wish" pricing because either they believe the product will drive business for a higher margin product, or they believe that "pay as you wish" pricing can yield more than conventional pricing—or both, for Radiohead.

Others, particularly some restaurants, price on this basis as a political statement, which can yield noneconomic benefits to the owners and perhaps yield some reputational gains in the community as well.

It might even improve the product by encouraging the waiter to provide excellent service. After all, the entire check, not just the tip, will be paid at the discretion of the customer. One consultant has described the business model as "an in-built quality control system."[25] Apparently, it's still working at Just Around the Corner: One recent reviewer of the restaurant noted that he has seen the same waitress at the restaurant for three years, which he says "must be a record in London."[26]

A final important element of some "pay as you wish" strategies, particularly in the music industry and perhaps in the emerging e-book industry, is the way it changes the cost structure. Refusing to set prices often cuts out a number of middlemen. For example, because publishers typically earn only 50% on the retail price of a book, voluntary payments by readers of a downloaded e-book produced at near-zero marginal cost don't need to be that high to generate a profit. For authors, who earn only 5% of a retail sale, the economics might be even more favorable.

Companies can also use such downloads to create a marketing buzz around a book. For example, Faber, a U.K. publisher, recently made historian Ben Wilson's book *What Price Liberty?* available for a free download six weeks before its paper publication—an experiment that Faber marketers believed would grow the audience for the book without cannibalizing hard-copy sales.[27]

In the textbook business, a "pay as you wish" model might have another advantage: It reduces the number of copies available for resale. A large percentage of textbooks students buy are used copies that the publisher and author earn no royalty on. As a result, a 100% "pay as you wish" model would help replace that profitless secondary market with one in which users would pay the publisher on an ongoing basis.

That's the theory. Whether a "pay as you wish" pricing strategy actually succeeds is another matter. In the music world, Radiohead members themselves have said that they don't believe "pay as you wish" pricing is something that could work for every group. They say that their success was primarily possible because they already had a large and established base of devoted fans. Similar experiments by lesser-known artists suggest that they might be right. Harvey Danger, a lesser-known band than Radiohead that still enjoys some fan recognition, released its album in 2005 under the same format as Radiohead. Fans downloaded the album 190,000 times, but only 1% of people paid something for it. Although the average donation (for those who donated) was $8.34, Harvey Danger's guitarist Jeff Lin says that it was "certainly not the runaway, huge financial bonanza some people thought it would be."[28]

However, other artists have experienced more success with "pay as you wish" pricing. In 2005, Canadian singer-songwriter Jane Siberry instituted what she referred to as "self-determined pricing" for her music downloads. At checkout, customers were given four options: pick a price, pay later after downloading the song, pay the standard 99¢, or "gift from Jane," which meant the customer did not have to pay.[29]

In the end, "pay as you wish" pricing may be an especially good way to price music and other experiential goods by focusing customers not on the price they will pay, but on the level of enjoyment they get from the song, book, or movie. Our colleague Peter Fader, a marketing professor at The Wharton School, argues that focusing

consumers on the price of an experiential good such as music ultimately pushes down the perceived value of the experience. "If you
boil it down to what is this song worth, you don't want people to be
thinking about that. This is one of the problems with the whole
iTunes business model, i.e., is it worth 99¢ or not? Music, being a
holistic good and an experiential good, is worth more than just the
bits that you are acquiring."[30]

Certainly, restaurateur Michael would agree with Fader that not
focusing customers on the price provides a greater potential upside
than conventional pricing. At Around the Corner, he said four American businessmen once came in for dinner and decided to leave £600
on the table when they left (nearly $1200 at the time). "They asked if
it was okay," the owner recalls. He answered, "'Of course.' If that's
what they thought it was worth, then fine!"[31]

The First Five Notes

Although music is a very risky business, we found that Radiohead's *In Rainbows* campaign shares the same five key qualities as
any successful "pay as you wish" pricing program:

1. A product with a low marginal cost
2. A fair-minded customer
3. A product that can be sold credibly at a wide range of prices
4. A strong relationship between buyer and seller
5. A very competitive marketplace

A Low Marginal-Cost Product

Shortly after the release of *In Rainbows*, Radiohead guitarist
Jonny Greenwood lost the password of some music software he uses,
and he e-mailed the developers to ask for a new password. "They
wrote back, 'Why don't you pay us what you think it's worth?'" Greenwood said.[32]

As Radiohead learned, software is also a good candidate for "pay as you wish" pricing. Our research suggests that any project with a low marginal cost—a high fixed cost for the first copy and low costs for each additional copy—is fair game.

For example, a dealership couldn't sell a car on a "pay as you wish" basis because the cost of a single nonpayment would outweigh the profit earned from dozens of buyers. Grocery stores would also not be good bets because most costs are marginal production costs. But software, music, and many other kinds of media and intellectual property typically have a low marginal cost. As the costs of these products are mostly fixed, the cost of selling an additional copy is quite low and often nearly zero online.

However, this does not mean that the marginal cost must be near zero for "pay as you wish" pricing mechanism to be viable. Restaurants have a substantial marginal cost, although fixed costs such as salaries and space leases are typically much greater than the marginal costs of food. At Around the Corner, the four American businessmen we mentioned earlier might have ordered a bottle of Château Mouton Rothschild Pauillac 2003, which may have cost £200, and yet in that instance "pay as you wish" still worked.

A Fair-Minded Customer

In the case of Radiohead, the success of *In Rainbows* relied on the fair-mindedness of the group's many dedicated fans. For a devotee of the band who has followed the band's development during the past 15 years, downloading without paying might be psychologically difficult.

Radiohead fans are apparently not alone in being fair-minded. Richard Thaler, a professor at the University of Chicago and a pioneering behavioral economist, has noted that by thinking of people as selfish, rational actors, classic economic theory has tended to overlook the fact that human beings actually often respond according to how they are treated. Many researchers have discovered that people tend to reciprocate "kindness with kindness, cooperation with cooperation, hostility with hostility, and defection with defection," Thaler says.[33]

Thaler also notes that people often act altruistically even without an economic incentive to do so. Even Adam Smith, the first modern theorist of capitalism, noted as far back as the Eighteenth Century:

> [H]ow selfish soever man may be supposed to be, there are evidently some principles in his nature, which interest him in the fate of others, and render their happiness necessary to him, though he derive nothing from it, except the pleasure of seeing it.[34]

"Pay as you wish" sellers seem to try to invoke this sense of fairness in their customers. For example, Radiohead forced buyers to enter an amount they wanted to pay before the download. Potential freeloaders had to enter £0 if they wanted to pay nothing. That action could trigger the fairness reflex: Is it fair of me to not pay anything for someone else's labor?

When a transaction occurs in a social setting, such as a restaurant, the fairness reflex can be encouraged by creating a situation in which it is difficult for customers to not pay anything without some damage to their reputation—a process Erica Okada, assistant professor of marketing at the Michael G. Foster School of Business, calls "social monitoring."[35] For example, at the Ten Thousand Buddha House, a successful "pay as you wish" restaurant in Hong Kong, all diners must make reservations in advance, reducing the sense of anonymity.[36] Whoever is paying the bill won't want to lose face by looking cheap in front of others at their table—or even strangers in the restaurant.

Sometimes organizations that use "pay as you wish" pricing further discourage underpayment by trying to add to the payer's embarrassment. Just Around the Corner discourages underpayment by shaming the under-payer. "With these people who pay a silly amount, we give them their money back," says owner Michael.[37] Technically, the customer can get away with paying nothing, but for most people, a free meal at the cost of public humiliation is too expensive. Such episodes are a one-time loss for the restaurant and normally a one-time lesson for the customer. The deadbeat customer either writes a larger check and pays more at subsequent visits, or he never returns.

This kind of confrontation seems common to "pay as you wish" businesses. Sam Lippert, owner of the "pay as you wish" Java Street Café in Kettering, Ohio, makes customers pay him directly. "Well, you know, they have to look me in the eye and say that that's what they think is fair. And, you know, that's a big incentive. When someone's at the counter and you say, 'You get to pay what you think is fair,' very few people are going to take advantage of that situation," he says—"especially if you know them by their first name."[38]

Businesses use other mechanisms to make it easier for customers to follow their own best instincts. Farmers around Ithaca, New York, often leave tables filled with produce on the side of the road, along with a cash box. They reduce their customers' temptation to run off with the money by making it difficult to remove the box or to take money out of the box's narrow piggy-bank slit. The behavioral economists who wrote about their business model note that they think the farmers have human nature figured out: "They feel that enough people will volunteer to pay for the fresh corn to make it worthwhile to put it out there. The farmers also know that if it were easy enough to take the money, someone would do so."[39] As an old Chinese saying goes, the lock on a door is meant to prevent the theft by a gentleman, not by a thief.

A strong sense of community among customers seems to help build this sense of social pressure as well. During the October downloads, many Radiohead fans reportedly asked each other how much they paid for their "free" downloads. The fact that "pay as you wish" restaurants have done well both in upscale urban neighborhoods and rural coffee shops suggests that "pay as you wish" pricing might be most effective in places with a strong sense of community.

But even in more hectic, impersonal situations, social monitoring seems to have some effect. For example, paying nothing at the Metropolitan Museum requires "buying" a lapel button directly from a museum employee, creating an uncomfortable social context for the visitor—in addition to the real or imagined social pressure exerted by others who have paid and, perhaps, by their own family.

New ways to create social pressure online may develop in the future as well. Wessex Press, the publishing house that publishes Capon's textbook, *Managing Marketing in the 21st Century,* tells customers that they can download the book for free, but they must "agree to receive an e-mail from Wessex in a few months' time encouraging you to pay what *Managing Marketing in the 21st Century* was worth to you."[40]

Far from underpaying, certain "pay as you wish" situations lead customers to err on the high side. For example, people at Just Around the Corner in London reportedly pay 10%–20% more than they normally would for an equivalent meal. When a pricing mechanism appeals to customers' good side, it can bring the best out of the customers.

A Wide Distribution in the Amount Customers Are Willing to Pay for a Product

The fact that some people care about Radiohead more than others was another reason for the campaign's success. If a product's perceived value doesn't vary much, encouraging customers to set their own prices might not be profitable. Much of the profit in "pay as you wish" pricing lies in the wide distribution of customers who don't know the underlying cost structure and overestimate the actual cost. A wide distribution of willingness to pay also makes it more profitable to charge different customers different prices. "Pay as you wish" pricing enables the seller to achieve price discrimination tailored to individual customers.

A Strong Relationship Between Buyer and Seller

After people have established a relationship, whether it is a one-sided relationship with a group such as Radiohead or a more mutual relationship with a salesperson, they often feel a need to reciprocate their kindness. Many businesses with conventional pricing have incorporated this tendency into their customer service practices—from Nordstrom, the high-end U.S. department store famed for providing extraordinary levels of service, such as gift-wrapping packages bought at other stores, to Wal-Mart, the low-price zealot that installs a person at every entrance, often a friendly old lady. Whether the idea is called "aggressive hospitality," as Wal-Mart founder Sam Walton branded his approach to customer service,[41] or an injunction to their employees to "think like the customer," the underlying idea is the same.[42] And in the case of the Wal-Mart greeter, the aim is not only to encourage loyalty, but also to discourage theft.[43]

The same principle may be even more important in "pay as you wish" pricing because the decision to leave anything is a voluntary act. If a waiter has been kind and helpful, it's difficult to walk away from a meal without tipping, although diners aren't legally obligated to leave anything.

Framing devices, such as the general custom in the United States of tipping 15% or the Metropolitan's posted notice about a suggested donation for admission, also add pressure to pay more than a token amount. Such frames might be a useful tool in "pay as you wish" pricing, which otherwise forces consumers to do more of the work involved in setting the price.

Getting to know how customers decide what to pay can also help a seller effectively implement "pay as you wish" pricing. Most consumer behavior studies suggest that buyers use three ways to decide the price they are willing to pay: anchor pricing, value pricing, and fair pricing.

When customers use anchor pricing (sometimes called reference pricing), they compare the price of similar goods to determine a price.

For example, users might note that CDs on iTunes sell for an average of $13 or recall that the price of a previous Radiohead CD is $15, which sets an upward boundary for the price they will pay. They might reason that if a CD downloaded from iTunes costs $13, and perhaps $9 ends up going to the label, Apple, and other marketing expenses, the artist might end up with $4.[44] As Radiohead doesn't have a label or other marketing expenses, they might conclude that $4 would be a fair price for their new CD.

A second common strategy customers use is value pricing—deciding the value the album represents to them and then using that as the maximum price they would be willing to pay to own the CD. For example, on Salon.com, user Sponte comments, "[I paid] £10...so, roughly $20 U.S.—since it's whatever I want to pay and that I value Radiohead as an artist and applaud this experiment...."[45]

In the third strategy, fair pricing, customers try to determine what they consider a "fair" price, their intuitive idea of what sounds like a fair return for the seller. Consider what these users at Salon.com say they paid for *In Rainbows:*

> "I decided to pay £5. I think $10 sounds about fair for a record these days."—User Ozoneon
>
> "I am preordering the album for £3. Sounds fair to me."—User edsohsmith[46]

Each of these methods relies to an extent on preexisting knowledge or sentiments to help anchor the price, which suggests that a radically new product might be difficult to sell using "pay as you wish." Knowing that the going rate for downloading a song is 99¢, or that a cup of coffee is generally a dollar or two, informs the customer's understanding of what an item is "supposed" to cost. Without an anchor price or a clear understanding of the value of a product's advantages, a customer would likely have a hard time deciding what the "fair price" should be.

A Competitive Marketplace

The music industry is very competitive, not only because of the number of bands that compete for young fans' devotion, but also because of piracy that tempts those young fans not to pay anything for songs. In this marketplace, given the alternative of a band setting a fixed price and seeing only a few people buying, "pay as you wish" can be a superior pricing mechanism even if the band's objective is to maximize its profitability.

Indeed, in a very competitive marketplace anywhere, "pay as you wish" may very well be an effective way for competing firms to avoid ruinous price competition. When consumers pay what they wish, prices in the market become autonomous, and competing firms no longer set any prices. When they do not set prices, they cannot and will not compete on prices!

Conclusion

"Pay as you wish" pricing probably goes back to the roots of trade, to the days when value was even more difficult to assign than it is in today's cash economy. Then, as now, "pay as you wish" pricing served as a good way not only to transfer goods and services, but also to build a stronger sense of community. It's easy to imagine within a family or a village that such large webs of mutual obligation could end up feeling virtually indistinguishable from good deeds.

As the collective wisdom of many cultures suggests—from the English proverb that "the giving hand, gets" to the Chinese injunction that if "if somebody gives you one drop of benefit, you should repay it with a spring of kindness"—human beings seem hard-wired for positive reciprocity. In the end, it's possible that "pay as you wish" may sometimes be not only a convenient process for exchanging goods and services, but also an elemental way in which communities are built or strengthened.

Certainly, Radiohead seems to have experienced the sales of its album this way—as a kind of affirmation from its fans. "It released us from something," says Yorke, the band's leader. "It wasn't nihilistic, implying that the music's not worth anything at all. It was the total opposite. And people took it as it was meant. Maybe that's just people having a little faith in what we're doing."[47]

Or as Hufford, the band's manager, put it, "People made their choice to actually pay money. It's people saying, 'We want to be part of this thing.' If it's good enough, people will put a penny in the pot."[48]

Endnotes

[1]Adler, Heather, "Radiohead Spurns Label of Digital Crusaders," *The Star Phoenix* (February 27, 2008): C6.

[2]Byrne, David, "David Byrne and Thom Yorke on the Real Value of Music," *Wired* (December 18, 2007): http://www.wired.com/entertainment/music/magazine/16-01/ff_yorke.

[3]Gibson, Owen, "The Megas...Innovators of the year winner: Bryce Edge and Chris Hufford." *The Guardian* (10 March 2008): Supplement, 17.

[4]Pareles, Jon, "Pay What You Want for This Article" *International Herald Tribune* (December 13, 2007): 6.

[5]Gibson, 17.

[6]Byrne, *Wired*.

[7]www.cnn.com/2007/SHOWBIZ/Music/10/10/radiohead.reader.feedback/index.html. (We have no way of knowing if the payment is made.)

[8]www.time.com/time/arts/article/0,8599,1572805,00.html.

[9]http://online.wsj.com/article/SB118824546924410128.html?mod=hps_us_editors_picks.

[10]www.restaurant.org/pressroom/pressrelease.cfm?ID=1010.

[11]Levy, Bergen, et al., "Menu Costs, Posted Prices, and Multiproduct Retailers," *Journal of Money, Credit, and Banking* (November 1999): 686.

[12]"Tackling the Textbook Giants," Columbia Business School "Public Offering" blog (October 15, 2008).

[13]*Ibid.*

[14]*Ibid.*

[15]Cardew, Ben, "A year of few successes," *Music Week* (January 12. 2008): 3.

[16]Ben Sisario, "Pop Tours Still Sell, Despite Economy," *New York Times* (July 12, 2008): http://query.nytimes.com/gst/fullpage.html?res=9904E5DE1F31F931A25754C0A96 E9C8B63&sec=&spon=&pagewanted=print.

[17]Lewis, Randy "Making Nice Pays Off for the Police," *Los Angeles Times* (January 5, 2008): http://www.latimes.com/entertainment/la-et-ultimate5jan05,1,3741559.story

[18]Mary Ellen Podmolik, "Rocking On, Lollapalooza-Style...," *Chicago Tribune* (April 8, 2008): http://archives.chicagotribune.com/2008/apr/08/business/chi-tue_ lollapaloozaapr08.

[19]www.time.com/time/arts/article/0,8599,1666973,00.html.

[20]*Ibid.*

[21]http://online.wsj.com/article/SB118824546924410128.html?mod=hps_us_editors_ picks.

[22]http://seattletimes.nwsource.com/html/businesstechnology/2003558690_terra-bite06e.html.

[23]John Roberts, "Café Owner Thrives with No-Pricing Policy," *CNN* (March 17, 2009): http://www.cnn.com/2009/US/03/17/lippert.qanda/index.html.

[24]Ben Pappas, "Transparent Eyeball," *Forbes* (September 20, 1999): http://www. forbes.com/forbes/1999/0920/6407047a.html.

[25]Imogen Wall, "It May Be a Dog-Eat-Dog World, but Dining Here Won't Prove It," *The Wall Street Journal* (December 11, 1998): B1.

[26]www.thelondonrestaurantreview.co.uk, review by "Olivier."

[27]Lea, Richard, "Faber Launches 'Pay-What-You-Want' Ebook," *The Guardian* (March 9, 2009):

[28]http://online.wsj.com/article/SB119211424892356048.html.

[29]http://music.yahoo.com/read/news/26558598.

[30]http://knowledge.wharton.upenn.edu/article.cfm?articleid=1821.

[31]Imogen Wall, "It May Be a Dog-Eat-Dog World, but Dining Here Won't Prove It," *The Wall Street Journal* (December 11, 1998): B1.

[32]Pareles, Jon, "Pay What You Want for This Article" *International Herald Tribune* (December 13, 2007): 6.

[33]Robyn Dawes and Richard Thaler, "Anomalies: Cooperation," *Journal of Economic Perspectives* 2, no. 3 (Summer 1988): 190.

[34]Dawes and Thaler, quoting Smith's *Theory of Moral Sentiments*, 192.

[35]http://seattletimes.nwsource.com/html/businesstechnology/2003558690_terra-bite06e.html.

[36]www.springwise.com/food_beverage/paywhatyouwant_restaurants/.

[37]Ben Pappas, "Transparent Eyeball," *Forbes* (September 20, 1999): http://www.forbes.com/forbes/1999/0920/6407047a.html.

[38]John Roberts, "Café Owner Thrives with No-Pricing Policy," *CNN* (March 17, 2009): http://www.cnn.com/2009/US/03/17/lippert.qanda/index.html

[39]Dawes and Thaler, 191.

[40]Managing Marketing in the 21st Century website, www.mm21c.com.

[41]Michael Berdahl, *What I Learned from Sam Walton: How to Compete and Thrive in a Wal-Mart art World* (NJ: Wiley, 2006).

[42]Spector, Robert et al., *The Nordstrom Way to Customer Service Excellence: A Handbook for Implementing Great Service in Your Organization* (New York: Wiley, 2005).

[43]*Ibid.*

[44]www.time.com/time/arts/article/0,8599,1666973,00.html.

[45]http://letters.salon.com/tech/machinist/blog/2007/10/01/radiohead/view/index5.html?show=all.

[46]*Ibid.*

[47]Byrne, *Wired*

[48]Pareles, Jon, "Pay What You Want for This Article" *International Herald Tribune* (December 13, 2007): 6.

2

Why the Best Things in Life Are Free

"We have to look at today's economy and say, 'What is it that's really scarce in the Internet economy?' And the answer is attention."

Hal Varian, Chief Economist of Google and Professor of Information Sciences, Business, and Economics at University of California at Berkeley

Imagine you are the marketing manager of a diversified services company. Thanks to advanced technology, some of it proprietary, your company can deliver information in a moment that would once have taken thousands of people thousands of hours to research, including the content of millions of books and scholarly papers. You also make it easy for people all over the world to organize and swap their photos, translate documents to and from 40 different languages, track their investments, send email, and even create documents on some fairly complex word-processing software. Through another division, you enable them to watch bits of virtually any film or television show they can remember and post their own videos for the entire world to see. You have even made it possible for people to look at their own backyard from space.

Now for the trillion-dollar question: How much should you charge for all this? Some of the individual lines, such as the photo storage or the office products, could cost hundreds of dollars. Others, such as spy satellite photos, might just be curiosities, but still worth something to a select audience. Taken together, however, the value of the whole suite would be thousands of dollars, if not, as Visa likes to say, priceless.

In fact, priceless is exactly the price Google has chosen. As far as consumers are concerned, access to the powerful search computers behind Google.com, which have made so many lives easier and better, is absolutely free to anyone who wants to log on.

Maybe for growing volume, free makes sense, but now that it's the world's dominant search engine, why does Google stick with this model? It's not because Sergey Brinn, one of the young co-founders, was born in the old Soviet Union and is nostalgic for communism. Nor because the company shares the utopian idea of some of the early Internet developers that information somehow needs to be free.

The real reason becomes apparent after a visit to Google's headquarters at Mountain View, California. From the entrance, Google's headquarters looks like a lot of other corporate headquarters, or campuses, as they're often called these days: bright, cheerful, vaguely collegiate. But that's where the similarities end.

Like Google customers, Google employees get a lot of freebies. That's part of the reason *Fortune* rated Google the best company to work for in the United States in 2008. Google employees take home not only the usual corporate benefits, such as health plans and stock options, but also a variety of unusual ones, including access to a free restaurant, free onsite massages, free yoga classes, and free haircuts. Google even offers free laundry service, to make sure their busy workers have clean clothes. The whole atmosphere feels like a first-class university, only better. In fact, the company is so helpful that an employee might never want to leave.

Which is sort of the point. Google offers generous benefits because managers have decided that these freebies encourage their employees to stay longer and work better. Longer, better hours mean more productivity—and, eventually, more productive employees mean more revenue for the company.

Of course, the same is true on a much larger scale for Google the search engine: The more value Google gives away, the more it seems to get in return. Like the pampered nerds of Mountain View, Google users pay for all the good things Google gives them with their time and attention. Their loyalty creates an immensely valuable audience for Google, which sells their attention to advertisers, who form the second side of Google's primary market.

These days, the market values Google at about $106 billion (which sounds like a lot until you consider that the company earned $21 billion in revenue in 2008), $13 billion of that in gross profit. It's a remarkable number, especially considering how many businesses floundered in 2008 and early 2009, when even the most established and diversified blue chips had a hard time generating profits. General Electric cut its dividend for the first time since 1938. Warren Buffett's equally diversified conglomerate, Berkshire Hathaway, reported a 96% drop in earnings in the fourth quarter of 2008. But throughout the turmoil, Google's earnings held steady and even beat expectations, generating $1.8 billion in free cash flow, even though probably 99% of its customers never pay a dime.

To paraphrase Gordon Gekko, the evil *Wall Street* movie tycoon, free is good—free works.

But how? It's easy to say, "Simple, advertising," but it's more complicated than that. Plenty of other enterprises didn't succeed with advertising over the same period. What makes Google different is that, unlike almost all past mass media giants, Google delivers entirely tangible value to its advertising customers. Not so much because the audience is a vast mass audience, but because it's a vast collection of individuals with distinct, known preferences. On any given day, nearly 32% of Internet users worldwide use Google, according to Alexa—that's roughly 500 million people. Millions of others see ads served by Google on other websites. Each of those individuals is reached—particularly if making a query—at a moment when, by the nature of the medium, the item on the screen is top-of-mind. People might watch television they don't care about, or they might flip through newspapers and not find anything interesting, but they don't make Internet searches on topics about which they have no interest.

This combination of scale and specificity makes Google an almost perfect medium for marketers. Unlike a typical advertiser, the Google keyword client pays only when potential customers have clicked on a link on the search engine or a banner ad that took them to their site. Google advertising clients get their own freebies, too: Besides not paying for uninterested consumers, as they would have in most old media models, they don't have to pay any more than the market-clearing price for access to their leads because Google sets the cost of each keyword by auction. For instance, advertising displayed alongside a search for the keywords "marketing consultant" currently runs at $4 per click-through, while "price consultant" is available at the bargain rate of $2.89.

Home of the Free

Google's situation is special but not unique. These days, "free" strategies are booming. Many companies—and not just technology companies—have worked out free strategies that seem to serve them well in building and keeping a customer base. In fact, free strategies are now so popular that they are being thought of as more than a pricing strategy. Whole books have been written on what some commentators have dubbed the "Freeconomy."

Of course, there is no free economy any more than there is a free lunch. There may be many free riders, but in the end, someone pays. In technical terms, the free economy is usually based on what economists call a two-sided market, in which the seller has two kinds of customers and wouldn't have a business without both sets. A classic example is Ladies' Night at a bar, which charges men for their drinks but serves women for free. Fewer men would turn up without the women, and men don't seem to pinch pennies when it comes to having a chance to mingle with women in bars.

But that's a very simple example. The reality is a bit more complex. Perhaps the easiest way to understand the ins and outs of pursuing a free strategy is to look at the factors driving the current free economy boom.

The biggest driver of today's boom is, of course, the decline in the marginal cost of information. Huge advances in information technology have been made over the last 15 years. In 1995, for example, review guides to the Internet sometimes included injunctions not to waste bandwidth. The Internet was for scholars who had valuable things to say to each other, guides scolded, not *Star Trek* fans. Rapid advances in computer power have changed all that. Today ordinary people send valuable and not-so-valuable information to each other all over the world for next to nothing. Computing power, too, has grown exponentially—and gets cheaper every year, whether the task is to manipulate data or store it. The idea of limited capacity online now seems almost absurd, akin to worrying about running out of electricity when you switch on a light.

In the view of Hal Varian, Google's chief economist and a professor of economics at Berkeley, most of the free boom is a direct consequence of the growth of cheap digital media. "The content is as valuable as it ever was; it's just the competition that's pushed the prices down to something that approximates zero," he says. "So it's not something that the content producers necessarily embrace, but it's something they're forced into by the nature of the technological change."[1]

The growth of the Internet itself has also been conducive to free offers by creating a mass audience for all this content. Whereas 12 years ago only a few million people were online, now nearly 1.6 billion use the Internet regularly, making it possible to reach hundreds of millions of people at nearly the same cost it once took to reach thousands.

However, the more important value, as Google has found, is not the fact that the Internet has aggregated a new mass audience, but that it has aggregated millions of different audiences.

Crowd-sourcing is a second factor driving costs down. The ability of users to participate in the creation of intellectual property is having a dramatic impact on the costs of information and entertainment. Consider YouTube. Founded only four years ago and acquired by Google in 2006 for $1.76 billion in stock, YouTube has grown into the world's largest video library almost overnight. Today it's the fourth-most-popular site on the Internet. About 20% of all Internet users access it every day, with 20 hours of additional content added every minute.[2] The cost for producing all that content? Again, priceless: YouTube doesn't produce any of those millions of hours of video content. Amateurs provided virtually all the clips in the beginning and even now contribute most of it, although increasing amounts of content are pirated or licensed clips from TV shows, music videos, and movies. Outside of the considerable costs of hosting—estimated at more than $1 million a day—Google spends almost nothing creating the content.

A new kind of amateur journalism created by thousands of amateur reporters is also creating value. CNN's i-reporter program builds on the news-gathering efforts of thousands of amateur TV reporters. The Huffington Post, a popular liberal website, is also remarkably lean, staffed by a handful of full-time reporters, a gaggle of celebrity columnists, and more than 3,000 volunteers. Incredibly, in spite of being run on a relative shoestring, the Huffington Post has a circulation of 1.6 million a day, almost double what Washingtonpost.com is able to do with a staff of hundreds of professionals.[3]

Nor is the rough draft of history the only one amateurs are writing these days. Amateur reference-book writers have completely undermined the traditional reference book business. *Encyclopaedia Britannica* is still publishing and maintains print, online, and DVD versions, but it faces a huge uphill battle against such upstarts as the crowd-sourced Wikipedia. The print edition of the 65,000-article encyclopedia sells for $1,149, DVD versions sell for $24.95, and a one-year subscription to Britannica Online sells for $35.95. Wikipedia, on the other hand, is free.

To make matters worse for Britannica, Wikipedia is a better product for most people's purposes. Teachers may still rail against the volunteer-written Wikipedia for unreliability, but a survey by the British science magazine *Nature* found that it was actually only a little less reliable than the old standard, with four errors for every three in Britannica.[4] But worst of all for Britannica, Wikipedia is not only free, it's much more comprehensive: Wikipedia has 2.1 million articles to Britannica Online's 120,000,[5] an investment that Britannica can in no way match. "I don't see a way out for content that competes directly with Wikipedia at this point," says a writer of a print guide to Wikipedia. "They can't compete with an infinite talent pool. And it's current."[6]

As a practical matter, the idea that the two are still competing in any meaningful way is absurd. On any given day, roughly 8% of Internet users worldwide visit Wikipedia.org. Alexa rates it the seventh-most-popular site worldwide. Britannica Online, by contrast, usually comes in at around 3,000th.

Social networking sites—which now have hundreds of millions of members and require very little content to sustain themselves—are another kind of crowd-sourced content that's providing cheap entertainment to millions. Such sites create a huge source of value and an equally huge source of new competition for retailers and entertainment producers. Teenagers still get just as excited by pop songs and movies as they ever did, but when it comes down to a choice between watching a music video or chatting on Facebook with that cute girl in Algebra II, Facebook wins every time.

Outside the Internet, free is also becoming increasingly popular partly because in a world of cluttered messages, "free" stands out. Its advertisements might get lost, but when Ben & Jerry's gives away ice cream, the lines can extend around the block. One successful West Coast restaurant chain, The Cheesecake Factory, gives away a lot of cheesecake whenever it opens a new location. Established outlets also give customers a lot of food, too (another kind of freebie): huge portions that ensure that 80% of the clientele walk out the door with a bag of leftovers. "It doesn't hurt to have people walk around with the bags," explains Howard Overton, Vice President of Business Development and Marketing.[7]

Freebies are also strategically used as loss-leaders, although typically more on a short-term promotional basis. In summer 2008, for example, during the oil price spike, a number of stores in Florida offered customers cards for free gas with every $50 purchase. The promotion worked well for many participants. Sweetbay Supermarket, a grocery store in Sarasota, offered a gas voucher for every $50 purchased. Customers could trade six vouchers for one $50 card. The upshot: The store issued 1,400 gas cards, and its sales rose by $70,500. So did gas sales, ironically: In spite of the giveaway, gas sales rose 45%.[8] Nor was Sweetbay alone. Other kinds of companies, from shoe stores to banks to apartment management companies, ran similar gas-related promotions.

The final element of the growth of the free economy is the peculiar power of zero to grow volume. As a price, zero has some obvious limitations, but from the marketer's point of view, zero is the next best thing to paying someone to take a product away. Often zero seems to act as a demand-booster—even when the price of a product has been marked down from a penny.

Interestingly, customers actually prefer products that cost nothing to those for which they paid a few cents. Scholars at Massachusetts Institute of Technology conducted a series of experiments to try to measure just how much people liked something free. In one of the most dramatic, they asked 60 people to choose between buying a Hershey's Kiss, which they could buy for 2¢, buying a higher-quality Ferrero chocolate for 27¢, or buying nothing. A total of 40% chose Ferrero, 45% chose Hershey, and 15% chose nothing. When the price was moved 1¢—the Ferrero for 26¢ and the Hershey's Kiss for

1¢—only 40% chose Hershey. But when the price dropped one more penny, to 25¢ for Ferrero and free for the Kiss, 90% took them up on the free offer, and only 10% bought the Ferrero.[9]

This preference for zero is so strong that it can drive demand even when the free price is bundled with something of much larger value. For example, when Amazon rolled out a free shipping offer in Europe, it once mistakenly forgot to include France and instead left the price at a negligible rate, the equivalent of 10¢. The result: In most countries, orders rose dramatically. But not in France.[10]

Why do people care so much about a few pennies? It could be that people just respond to a bargain: The discount on the 26¢ chocolate was just a few percentage points down, while the 2¢ candy was marked down by 100%. However, Shapanier and others believe there is actually something special about the goose egg. They suggest three possible explanations. First is social norms. People look at free things as a kind of a gift and think of them more charitably than they do a regular product. Certainly, there seems to be some element of truth to this. Gifts have long been a part of commerce. Think of cups of tea in the bazaar or the baker's dozen. Although English bakers began the practice of the baker's dozen simply as a way to avoid running afoul of tough Thirteenth Century laws that regulated the weight of bread loaves, the practice has long since evolved into a loyalty gift in the United States. Second, these analysts suggest that people have trouble setting prices themselves. When people are unsure about how to value two choices, consumers will conclude that whereas the 25¢ chocolate may or may not be good, free chocolate will definitely be better than nothing. Finally, researchers say that people naturally prefer options with no downside, and for consumers, zero is an offer that's hard to refuse.

Live Free or Die?

For the Britannicas of this world, the fight against a product that is at once cheaper and arguably better seems not just uphill, but impossible. As we saw in Chapter 1, "'Pay As You Wish' Pricing," the music industry has had to rethink its model entirely as it watched CD sales slip from $13 billion in 2001 to $7 billion today, even as online sales grew by only $1.5 billion.[11] Traditional software makers are also under attack. In response to the growing number of free online versions of basic office applications such as word processing and spreadsheets created by Google, Open Office, and others—domains in which the Microsoft Office suite held a near monopoly for the better part of three decades—Microsoft recently announced that it intends to produce its own free, web-based versions. Already "Mister Softee" is offering a 60-day free trial for users of its Office products and, at certain times of the year, gives students a $60 downloadable version of its premium version of Office, which normally sells for around $460.[12] Some analysts even see Microsoft's courting of Yahoo! in 2008 as an admission that a business driven by software licenses is on its way out. "If Microsoft had to start over today, it wouldn't even think about charging money for its software," says Yun Kim, an industry analyst with Pacific Growth Equities. "Nobody in their right mind is developing a business in the consumer market to charge [for software]."[13]

The "free" challenge that information and service companies face might prove even more serious than the "China price" Western manufacturers faced this past decade. A company facing a fast-growing nonprofit competitor such as Wikipedia or a low- or no-cost platform such as Craig's List typically finds itself in trouble not unlike the kind Western manufacturers have faced, only worse. The collapse of U.S. manufacturing took years, and that was against competition that sold at 30%–50% off. Imagine how long the typical store would last if the Martians landed, opened a saucer-shaped store down the street with better stock, and marked everything in the shop as "free." Even if people had positive associations with the old ways of doing things, and even if they believed that the company served some other valuable role in society, it wouldn't take long for them to feel right at home in the saucer.

To make matters worse for a paid contender, many freebies are designed to lock customers into a particular design, a variation on the famous Gillette razor blade strategy. This model seems particularly well-suited for software, as switching costs in changing systems can be high. Some developers are already building this dependency into the business model. For example, some open-source software companies give away the program but charge for the support. Perhaps as a countermove to such "free" competition, Microsoft recently unveiled a program called BizSparks that provides free software to startup companies for up to three years, after which the customer must find new systems or become a paying buyer. Offline, the same model is also interesting other kinds of technology start-ups as well: Better Place, a startup electric car company, reportedly plans to sell its cars for very little and instead make its money on batteries.[14]

For a company that's been in business for more than a few minutes, developing a free business model is not easy. As the Microsoft example suggests, however, fighting free competition is difficult, but not impossible.

Certainly, free is a hard price to beat. To beat free, you essentially need to pay customers to use your product or service for a limited period of time. However, the moment you start doing that, you will find cottage industries springing up in which people will be hired, probably from China or India, to use the product or service as an occupation. The only choice left then is to match the zero price. However, for most companies, matching zero is not an option because the cost structures of the competitor are radically different, and the institutional change required to make the shift to a free model is too great. Lowering prices also can't do more than prolong the agony; as we have seen, there is all the difference in the world between free and nearly free. Unless the quality is absolutely abysmal, a credible free competitor will almost always outflank the paying player on volume.

But marketers caught in this situation have other options besides dusting off their resumés. It is crucial to keep in mind that free is just another pricing strategy. "Free" has some magical powers, it's true, but Google's two-sided business model isn't undefeatable unless you try to fight it on its own terms. When you accept free as the norm and cannot think of anything else to do, you've already lost the game.

The challenge currently facing the newspaper industry is a good example of why you can't fight free with free. Newspapers are caught in a terrible bind today. More young readers get their news online, mostly from free sources. Fewer papers being read makes the medium less attractive to advertisers. The papers cut costs, which in turn, makes them less compelling to both groups. At the same time, advertising is migrating to the Internet with incredible rapidity, and newspapers are losing their traditional role in the community as what might be called the original virtual exchange, as a central hub for information about buying and selling various kinds of goods and services.

Twenty years ago, consumers used the newspaper to buy and sell their things and to look for cars, houses, and work. Today all those functions have gone online, and perhaps 40% of newspaper revenue has gone with them. Once the only real marketplace for all kinds of goods and services, the local newspaper today is just one of many—most of them free or nearly free. The newspaper industry's multibillion-dollar classified ad business is being replaced now by eBay; Google; and, maybe most of all, the largely free classified service of Craig's List, which has grown into what may be the world's first $5-billion, 25-employee company.

Most newspapers have tried to retain their audiences by offering readers free online news. This has been a popular success—some papers have more readers than ever—but not a financial one. For years, papers have tried to expand their online ad sales, but so far, the transition hasn't worked well. Tom Corbett, an equity analyst for Morningstar, has estimated that the revenue growth of online ads versus the loss of print advertising is running about 1.7¢ gained online for every $1 of print advertising lost.

With fewer ads and fewer readers, newspapers are now hemor-rhaging cash. The American Newspaper Association estimates that the country's biggest newspaper chains saw their earnings decline by an average of 198% in 2008. In one typical case, the Hearst Corpora-tion, owner of the San Francisco Chronicle, was faced with the task of trying to trim expenses that totaled 47% of its payroll. Newspaper publishing companies are scrambling to find something, anything, to staunch the red ink—cutting staff, outsourcing production operations to India, and consolidating editing operations into a single, central location. But none of these moves seems likely to do much more than buy a little more time.

What could they do instead? Defending against a "free" competi-tor requires clear-sightedness about the seller's sources of value. It requires openness to new kinds of value propositions that have arisen because of either advances in technology or changes in the competi-tive landscape. Finally, it demands a willingness to imagine a fresh role for itself in a changed world.

To borrow and extend an analogy recently put forth by *The Econ-omist*,[15] newspapers today are a bit like the grand department stores—the Lord & Taylors, the Wanamaker's, and others—that were once a focal point of every American city and are now mostly gone.

As *The Economist* noted, just because the department stores died doesn't mean people stopped shopping. In fact, they're shopping more than ever. It's just that their habits have changed. The shoppers have gone elsewhere, either to the big box stores that can offer lower prices, to the high-end boutiques that can provide more style or bet-ter quality, or to online merchants that can offer convenience. The last 20 years were good for Wal-Mart, but they were also good for Tiffany's and Amazon.

For news pricing, this means that perhaps the best way to suc-cessfully fight no price is to set a high price. A $150-a-year newspaper subscription or even a $50 subscription won't win against free. A $1,700-a-month Bloomberg terminal contract just might.

Of course, price by itself won't do the trick. The price must be backed by a compelling value proposition. In the case of Bloomberg, for example, that means access to a variety of up-to-the-nanosecond market data and analytics. In fast-moving financial markets, a trader needs to have an information advantage to stay ahead of the game. In the case of a newspaper, it might mean providing more, not less, in-depth information to readers who have a laser focus on a subject that they find of intense interest, such as a local sports team, hobbies, or coverage of a locally important industry.

To say that newspapers are the last vestige of the mass-marketing era is probably not a great exaggeration. A subscriber to a newspaper receives the same stack of paper every morning whether or not he wants to read all of it, and he is charged the same amount no matter how much or how little he reads. So far, papers have tried to compete mostly by slimming the product. Instead, newspapers could take the Bloomberg route: Instead of dumbing down the content for greater general appeal, they could try to boost the value provided to readers of different interests (sports, politics, hobbies, antique, education, and so on) and aim for customers focused on a particular subject, to whom it can provide in-depth analysis or reporting. This strategy would take advantage of newspapers' greatest strength: high-quality news-gathering and analysis from professional writers. Furthermore, readers with different interests should be allowed to pick and choose what content to receive and pay different prices for what they get.

Access to the inner workings of the organization might also be part of the value proposition. A Boston-based news startup focused on foreign news, GlobalPost, offers free news to most readers but special service to others for $199 a year. Membership in the Passport service "offers an entrée into GlobalPost's inner circle." Not only do Passport members get exclusive content, but they can also participate in conference calls with reporters and even have the right to suggest stories.[16]

Unlike the old top-down model in which editors decide what readers will read, Passport members play an unprecedented role in shaping the stories that get covered.[17] In some ways, this is nothing new. For example, *The Economist* has long run a conference division that caters to the desire of executives to feel "in the know." Meetings typically feature world leaders or captains of industry and often include commentary provided by *Economist* reporters. What is new, perhaps, is the recognition that this desire to be "inside" the actual magazine would itself have a value that might be traded upon. For a news organization, the recognition that the customer can play a productive role beyond simply sending in a subscription check is also novel.

Other kinds of community can also prove a source of value. The controlled circulation model some professional publications use—restricting subscriptions and giving them away to subscribers who meet a particular profile—could grow more important, perhaps by making more effort to prequalify readers from more specific demographics or making access to the publication itself a sort of outward sign of status, a kind of Black Card for the briefcase.

Such an opportunity to be part of this exclusive group can also be transformed into an important benefit. Just as buyers of some luxury cars are sometimes encouraged to participate in group rallies, the community aspect of sharing the same information source could become another important source of revenue. Colleges already do this with special-interest tours led by professors—surely well-known journalists could act as guides for something similar. A branded personality could sell specialized content, the way celebrity TV chefs merchandise their restaurants or cookbooks: Order today and get special talks for subscribers or access to a special newsletter. Other kinds of specialized groups could build small but profitable niches as well: Imagine, for instance, if Paul Krugman, Nobel Laureate and *New York Times* columnist, started a book club on economic subjects, endorsing particular books as Oprah's book club does, and then perhaps delivered by-subscription lectures about them. That's not everyone's cup of tea, perhaps, but it doesn't have to be. Similar opportunities might emerge for technology columnists, such as David Pogue or Walt Mossberg. Certainly, publications would need to take care to avoid compromising their function as critics, but they could still somehow leverage the level of enthusiasm their readers have for them.

Other kinds of cross-sales based on brand and reader demographics could have some potential. For example, *The Wall Street Journal* recently launched a new online wine store, wsjwine.com, a joint venture between the *Journal* and Direct Wines, a direct-to-consumer wine dealer. Online readers of the *Journal's* popular wine section are sent to another site, a site with a similar look and feel that sells high-quality discount wines.

Whatever experiments succeed, the newspaper of the future will look a lot different than it does now. Ultimately, its evolution may be a bit like that of the television networks. Thirty years ago, local news shows and national news shows coexisted, with almost all the programs carried on local stations affiliated with the national networks. The national network news shows were institutions, and it was hard to imagine a world without them. Then cable came along, and CNN and its imitators sprang up. Low-cost local news channels grew, too. News with a particular ideological slant, such as the conservative Fox News channel, also arrived. CNBC showed up as well, covering not so much business as the stock market, and reaching the public at a time when watching the market and playing the market became a national sport.

True, most of these alternatives have been free to users. However, it's not impossible to imagine that the business model might have turned out differently. In the end, how much the consumer is willing to pay depends on how much unique value the news provider can create—and how well it can articulate that value. At this point, what the future holds for newspapers is anyone's guess. As we march further into the information age, it is difficult to miss the irony: one of the primary sources of information of the last 150 years is becoming less relevant. However, the newspaper's extinction need not be inevitable.

Whatever happens to newspapers, we can say with some degree of certainty that for newspapers to survive in the land of free, they need to do two things well. First, they need to target the right customers with right information and services that are of vastly superior quality than those available elsewhere. In an age when information is freely available everywhere, the quality of information available on topics of central interest to the customer will become even more important, not less. Second, the distribution of newspapers, the same stack of papers delivered at a specific time to readers' door steps, has to adapt to new digital technologies to allow for flexible choices of content, flexible delivery time and means, interactivity, and personalized pricing.

Still No Free Lunch

Free can be a powerful strategy, but it's not magic.

The limits are the same as in ordinary pricing: Somewhere along the way, companies must make a profit. Even when costs are near zero, somebody somewhere or sometime later must pay to keep the product on the shelves. There is still no such thing as a free lunch. However, as we have seen in this chapter, modern technologies have added a few corollaries: There's no such thing as a free lunch, unless someone else picks up the tab—or the customer pays later for a more expensive dinner.

Theoretically, an airplane flight might be supported entirely by passengers' agreeing to subject themselves to a three-hour infomercial. But in the end, the in-flight infomercial won't be enough to keep the plane in the air any more than freebies will be able to sustain the economy. Sooner or later, freebies can exist only when the sponsor makes enough profit to pick up the entire tab. No matter how high-tech the transaction, there's no escaping the law of the free lunch. As Peter Drucker once said that profit is the price of survival. Sooner or later, all those chicken wings must be paid for by someone's beer.

Endnotes

[1]"Hal Varian on How the Web Challenges Managers," McKinsey Quarterly, Jan. 2009.

[2]Alexa.com, September 24, 2009.

[3]Quantcast.com, September 26, 2009.

[4]McNaughton, John, "Media: Wikipedia isn't perfect but it's very, very impressive...," *Observer* (7 October 2007).

[5]Bond, Gwenda, "Fighting Facts and Figures: Wikipedia's the Elephant...," *Publisher's Weekly* (May 12, 2008).

[6]*Ibid.*

[7]Kovsky, Ed, *The Idaho Business Review,* "Cheesy: What Can the Boise Cheesecake Factory Teach You About Marketing Strategy? Plenty" (December 25, 2006).

[8]Ray, Russell, *Tampa Tribune Business News,* "Hey There, Want Some Free Gas?" (July 9, 2008).

[9]Shampanier, Mazar, and Ariely, "Zero as a Special Price: The True Value of Free Products," *Marketing Science* (November 2007): 746.

[10]*Ibid.,* 757.

[11]"How about Free? The Price Point That Is Turning Industries on Their Heads," Knowledge@Wharton (March 4, 2009).

[12]Richtel, Matt, "Facing Free Software, Microsoft Looks to Yahoo!," *New York Times,* (February 9, 2008).

[13]*Ibid.*

[14]"How about Free? The Price Point That Is Turning Industries on Their Heads" Knowledge@Wharton, (March 4, 2009).

[15]"Tossed by a Gale" *The Economist,* (May 14, 2009).

[16]Hilton, Jodi, "A Web Site's For-Profit Approach to World News" *New York Times,* (March 22, 2009).

[17]Worldpost.com marketing materials.

3

The Art of Price Wars

"To fight and conquer all your battles is not supreme excellence; supreme excellence consists in breaking the enemy's resistance without fighting."
Sun Tzu, *The Art of War*

American marketing experts usually see price wars as a strategy of last resort—a choice for the truly desperate or the deeply crazed.[1] The price war is regarded as a kind of nuclear option, a quick way to not only destroy the competition, but also blow yourself up—and maybe even ruin the profitability of your industry forever. From the PeopleExpress airfare wars of the 1980s to various price-slashing schemes by mindless dotcoms in the late 1990s, plenty of evidence seems to support the conventional wisdom. As an old *Fortune* magazine article put it, "What are price wars good for? Absolutely nothing."[2] Faced with the possibility of a price war, most experts have long agreed that the best response is to just say *No:* "The best way to escape a damaging price war is *not* to jump into the fray at all."[3]

But somebody forgot to send the manual to the world's fastest-growing industrial power. During the past 15 years, hundreds of firms in China have fought large-scale price wars in a wide range of industries, including consumer electronics, home appliances, personal computers, mobile phones, telecommunications equipment, airlines, and, most recently, automobiles. Certainly, some campaigns have gone badly, as a Western observer would have predicted. However, a surprising number of companies have thrived despite aggressive plays in which they dropped their prices by as much as 50%. In some cases, companies have even advanced all the way from being one of a number of players in their own province to the world leader in a particular category, largely on the strength of a sustained campaign of price wars.

It's easy to dismiss their successes as the outcome of a kind of blind, Darwinian scramble in which a few lucky companies survived: It is possible to win at Russian roulette, too—at least for a few rounds. But that isn't what's happened. A closer look reveals that these companies knew exactly what they were doing. In fact, over the past 15 years, Chinese companies have reinvented the price war, transforming what had been a tactic of last resort into an art.

Why Chinese Businesses Like Price Wars

Despite the fact that Chinese-led price wars have become a familiar terror to Western marketers, many practitioners and pricing experts are still genuinely puzzled as to why Chinese businesses like to play such a dangerous game. "Why can't they just lower the price by 10% or even 20%?" many Western marketers moan. "That way, they could keep their damned price advantage and do much better for themselves, too."

It's a good question, but few marketing scholars have looked seriously for an answer. Western academics, journalists, and executives have all tended to see the Chinese-led price wars not as the outcome of a deliberate strategy, but as the invisible hand of the market at work—the inevitable result of low-cost goods flooding a high-priced market, a phenomenon *BusinessWeek* once called "the three scariest words in U.S. industry: the China price."[4] Although it's easy for a Westerner to look at shelf after shelf of low-priced Chinese goods and see value mindlessly destroyed, the truth is very different.

First, simply for cultural reasons, the Chinese may be more open to price wars than Western businesses. The Chinese tend to think of business competition in military terms. No one should be surprised that firms in a country where executives routinely draw strategic inspirations from Sun Tzu's ancient classic *The Art of War* might have a different perspective on price wars. Executives in China commonly talk about the business arena as the "battleground," and they aren't speaking metaphorically: The very word for strategy in Chinese, *zhanlue*, means "battle plans" or "combat strategies."

This mental link between business and war is not just a habit of the executive suite. The popular press has made heroes of some of the "generals" who have won price wars and given extensive coverage to some of their more celebrated battles. Make a keyword search of "price war" in one Chinese newspaper database, and you'll find more than 13,000 articles on the subject in the past decade, many of which characterize the executives who initiated the price war as courageous, decisive "generals."

However, the main reason Chinese marketing strategists wage price wars doesn't have anything to do with Sun Tzu or glory on the marketing "battlefield." It's because so many Chinese companies have learned that, when faced with either a broad field of young, hungry competitors in their home province or well-entrenched, better-financed competitors abroad, a price war can be a great way to shake out competition and build a commanding market share in a short period of time:

- In 1995, IBM, Compaq, and HP were the three best-selling PC brands in China, and they all looked invincible. Three years later, the top five PC brands in China were all locals who had fought their way up through price wars.
- In 1999, something similar began to happen to the mobile phone business. Motorola, Nokia, and other foreign brands dominated China's mobile phone market whereas local brands held less than 5% of the market. Four years later, after a series of intense price wars, the local brands held more than 50% of the market.

- In 2005, Chery, a local automobile company with only 10 years of history, launched several rounds of price wars and beat many global players to take the fourth-biggest market share in China. Now Chery might be preparing for a similar assault on the U.S. market.

How much of this success should we ascribe to strategy and how much to luck and pluck? A close look at two early price wars that took place in China in the 1990s—first among color television builders and second among microwave oven manufacturers—suggests that luck has had little to do with the price warriors' success. If Chinese companies are crazy when it comes to pricing, they're crazy like a fox.

Color TVs

In early 1996, China's color TV industry was highly fragmented. The country had 130 manufacturers. Most sold fewer than 120,000 units a year. Only 12 had annual sales of more than half a million units, and 4 of the 12 had annual sales of more than 1 million units. As a result, most manufacturers operated inefficiently and few could take advantage of economies of scale. However, the competitors all slogged along because local governments owned a vast majority of these companies and protected them within their local markets.

For ambitious TV company CEOs, this local support made the game both harder to lose and harder to win—harder to lose because of protection at home, but harder to win because the competition was also protected. Boxed in, TV manufacturers couldn't create greater scale economies either by entering other regional markets or by seeking mergers and acquisitions.

The potential for upward mobility to higher-end sales was also blocked. At the time, China's color TV market had two tiers. Foreign brands served the upper segment of the market and enjoyed a 20% price premium over local brands. Despite that premium, foreign brands—Japanese brands, in particular—still held a dominant position in China, especially in urban markets. Although the quality of domestic products was comparable to that of foreign brands, local brands generally competed with one another in the low-end market. People who owned an import seldom considered local brands.

Local TV manufacturers were also beginning to feel squeezed. In late 1995, despite provincial support and protection, large-scale smuggling of color TVs from abroad had begun to drag down prices. To make matters worse, import tariffs were slated to go down in 1996 from 60% to 50% for small-screen color TVs and from 65% to 50% for large-screen color TVs. Foreign manufacturers, lured by the sheer size of the market, were making huge investments inside China: All 10 of the world's largest TV manufacturers were rapidly expanding their local production. Analysts estimated that in two years' time, if the global manufacturers attained their announcements, capacity would grow to 10 million units. Experienced and well financed, these newcomers were expected to flood the market with high-quality goods produced by cheap domestic labor and drive out the local brands. One large global color TV manufacturer predicted that in three years' time, it would destroy Changhong, the largest local competitor.

But Changhong had other plans.

With 17 production lines concentrated in one place, Changhong ran the largest and most efficient color TV factory in China. Its capacity at that time was at least double that of the second-largest Chinese manufacturer. Changhong was also the largest manufacturer of many key TV components, such as plastic injections, electronic parts, and remote controls. As a highly vertically integrated company located in Sichuan, one of China's less developed regions, Changhong also enjoyed huge cost advantages and earned the highest profit margin of all domestic color TVs. The net profit margins for Changhong stood at nearly 20%, far ahead of most domestic rivals.

Despite being the strongest domestic TV manufacturer, Changhong was far from complacent. Changhong's CEO, Ni Runfeng, spent several months in late 1995 and early 1996 weighing alternative strategies to increase the company's market share. The top executives at the company, including Ni, talked with a number of pricing experts, carried out marketing surveys in various regions, and closely examined the survey data. Through these interviews, surveys, and analyses, they collectively came to a conclusion that would startle most Western marketers: They needed to launch a price war.

As risky as it sounds to Western ears, the logic was compelling. Domestically, a price war would put the small, inefficient domestic TV manufacturers between a rock and a hard place: They could either cut their price and suffer a significant loss of margin or maintain their price and suffer a significant loss of volume. In either case, they would have to struggle mightily to survive. Changhong's timing was also good because the rules of the game just changed. Beijing now was pushing the local governments that had previously backed these small players to tighten their fiscal policies. Provincial enthusiasm for propping up their local heroes would become even weaker if Changhong could inflict quick and costly damage.

A significant price cut would also put premium-price foreign competitors in a bind. If they stayed out of the fray, Changhong would gain market share. If they fought back, they would leave a lot of money on the table from their loyal high-end customers without enough increase in sales to offset their lost profit, ceding Changhong a cost advantage. Third, they would risk eroding their brand equity and undermining their brand image as a premium product. This was assuming the foreign giants even had time to decide whether to parry the blow. Changhong believed that, given their pricing structure and the need to get their home offices to approve such a major strategic decision—likely a lengthy process—many of the foreign companies would never even have the chance to respond.

Changhong had other reasons for confidence. It was the first color TV manufacturer to be listed on China's stock market. It enjoyed a high level of brand awareness and a high-quality image among domestic brands. It also had a lower cost structure compared to the local competition. Changhong had other advantages, too, of a more temporary nature. In early 1996, Changhong had an inventory of around one million units, with a total estimated value exceeding 2 billion RMB. Changhong's efficiency suffered because of the huge inventory. However, this ready supply of a large quantity of color TVs provided the ammunition Changhong would need to initiate a price war to boost sales volume.

At that moment, Changhong was also better prepared than any other domestic competitor to ramp up its production if demand surged as expected. As the largest domestic color TV manufacturer, Changhong had built a very close relationship with key component suppliers in the color TV industry. After it launched the war, Changhong could still count on reliable supplies of key components for its production. This was especially true for color TV kinescopes, a key component for color TVs, which were flooding the market at that moment. Eight local kinescope manufacturers in early 1996 had a combined 1.25 million units of inventory according to one estimate, and Changhong could tap a significant number of those units as it ramped up production.

Finally, in early 1996, China's color TV sales were on the verge of taking off. With a significant drop in the price of color TVs, the industry demand could expand significantly, and Changhong would be well-positioned to capture a major chunk of that new demand.

After careful analysis, Changhong executives concluded that it didn't need a huge price cut for a price war to be effective. A 10% cut would enlarge its price advantage against foreign brands to about 30% (before the price war, the price gap between local and foreign brands was around 20%) and put many domestic rivals in the red. The price cut was also affordable for Changhong, given its prewar 20% profit margin.

On March 26, 1996, Changhong fired the first shot, announcing a price reduction of 8%–18% for all its 17- to 29-inch color TVs, leading to price reductions ranging from 1,000 to 850 RMB.

The price war evolved mostly as Changhong had expected. All domestic TV manufacturers, especially the small ones, were shocked and angered by Changhong's price reduction. However, they reacted with hesitation. Initially, most local players decided to stay out of the fray. Most had been caught by surprise, as intended. They were not prepared for the price cut and were unsure how to respond. Many also underestimated the possible impact of a price war because different brands dominated different regions. Others, mostly state-owned enterprises (SOEs) such as Panda and SVA, had high costs per unit and a thin profit margin. They could not match an 8%–18% price cut. None of the four biggest domestic players (Konka, Panda, SVA, and Peony) followed suit until June 6, 1996, when Konka announced a price cut of up to 20%. Panda and Peony pinned their hope on government intervention instead, to stop Changhong's "reckless" pricing behavior. Panda's executives were also distracted with preparations for the company's initial public offering in Hong Kong in May 1996.

Foreign brands also responded to Changhong's price reduction as Changhong had predicted. Two of the leaders, Sony and Panasonic, decided to take the high road: They would focus on quality and functionality, not on price. Maybe this would have worked in a mature market where their brand names were established, but in fast-changing China, it turned out to be the wrong call.

Some domestic manufacturers reacted more thoughtfully to Changhong's price cut. TCL, a medium-size TV manufacturer at that time, was the first. On April 1, it announced a price cut of 120–300RMB. Xiahua, another medium-size player, announced a price cut of 10%. However, because of the capacity constraint and the shortage of key components, most of Changhong's rivals could cut prices for small TVs only.

Finally, as an added bonus, Changhong's decision to initiate the price war generated a barrage of publicity throughout the country, which had a very positive impact on its sales.

A few months into the price war, Changhong's overall market share increased from 16.68% to 31.64%, with its share in the 25-inch market jumping from 20.76% to 45.25%, and its share in the 29-inch market increasing from 14.37% to 17.15%. Big domestic manufacturers that did not try to match Changhong saw their market shares dwindle. Panda's market share dropped from 7.6% to 5.8%, and SVA's market share dropped from 5.5% to 2.6%. The more nimble benefited. Some medium-size local players, particularly TCL and Xiahua, that followed suit quickly with their own price cuts increased their market share by more than 2%. At the same time, the scores of all small domestic players (those with annual sales of less than 200,000 units) suffered. In the first quarter of 1996, China's 100 largest department stores carried 59 local brands. By April, this number dropped to 42, while the small players' combined market share dropped more than 15%.

Foreign brands suffered as well. Before the price war, imports and joint venture products accounted for 64% of the market. By the end of 1996, the market share of domestic products had grown from 36% to almost 60%. By 1997, 8 of the top 10 best-selling TV brands in China were Chinese. The top three color TV brands belonged to three local players, Changhong, Konka, and TCL, with market shares of 35%, 15%, and 10% respectively. Only two foreign brands, Panasonic and Philips, remained in the top ten, each with only 5% of the market.

Not surprisingly, the media made CEO Ni a national hero, a sort of General Patton in a business suit.

The Microwave Oven Industry

The experience of Galanz, a microwave oven manufacturer, also suggests that Chinese price wars are won by the savvy, not the lucky.

Less than 2% of Chinese urban households owned microwave ovens in 1995. A microwave oven was a luxury item, and the total unit sales in that year were about one million. The profit margins were very high for manufacturers at the time (30%–40%) and attracted an incredible number of new entrants to the industry. Between 1995 and 1996 alone, the number of microwave oven producers grew from 28 to 116.

Galanz had entered the microwave oven business in 1992. By 1994, the company had built a market share of 10%, about 100,000 units at that time. By 1995, the Guangdong company had won a market share of 25%, as shown in Table 3.1. Galanz had become a formidable competitor through a recruitment strategy that drew talent from all over China. It had purchased an advanced production line from Japan and was now well equipped to respond quickly to market changes and other new opportunities.

TABLE 3.1   Galanz's Sales Information for 1995—2003

Year	Sales Volume (in '000)	Local Market Share	Int'l Market Share
1995	200	25.1%	
1996	650	34.5%	
1997	2,000	47.6%	
1998	4,000	61.4%	15%
1999	6,000	67.1%	20%
2000	10,000	76.0%	30%
2001	12,000	70.0%	35%
2002	13,000	70.0%	40%
2003	16,000	68.0%	44%

The company's major competitor in 1996 was Whirlpool-Xianhua (W-X), a joint venture formed in May 1995 between Whirlpool and Xinhua, a sizable Chinese manufacturer. Whirlpool held the majority interest. In early 1996, Galanz and W-X each owned about 25% of the market share in the microwave oven market, far more than the other small manufacturers. However, relative to W-X, Galanz had a clear advantage: It was a more focused company with a streamlined decision-making process. Whirlpool, by contrast, was new to the Chinese market (it entered in late 1994) and still learning the ropes. It had four joint ventures in four different cities with four different Chinese partners in four different product categories (microwave ovens, air conditioners, refrigerators, and washing machines). Understandably, it encountered many problems in its varied China operations and could not pay sufficient attention to W-X. In addition, Whirlpool's head office in China, then its Asia-Pacific office, and finally its U.S. headquarters each had to ratify W-X's key decisions, a process that often took three months.

Despite the perceived advantages, executives at Galanz did not take the plunge until August 1996. Senior executives had long and heated debates on the risks and benefits of launching a price war. The majority of senior managers at the time opposed the price war strategy and preferred a safer strategy of maintaining the current high profit margins. In the end, the CEO made the call: He sided with the minority and ordered his team to prepare for war.

Although the company was certainly on a healthy growth trajectory, Galanz made the decision for a number of reasons. First, a significant number of Chinese households were ready to modernize their kitchens with the purchase of a microwave oven, along with other appliances. Strategists at Galenz realized that its focus on high-end households and high margins today could preclude the company's expansion into that vast new market tomorrow. They estimated that significant price reductions could increase sales by about 100%.

Second, as one of the largest manufacturers in China, Galanz saw an opportunity to reorganize the industry for sustainable future growth. Yu Yaochang, the vice president of Galanz, recalls that one of the purposes of the first price war was to consolidate the industry by marginalizing small, inefficient players before they had a chance to grow and also to discourage even more new entrants. Maintaining a high profit margin strategy, on the other hand, would encourage even more new entries and hide inefficiencies going forward.

Third, and perhaps most important, a well-planned and executed price war could help Galanz establish its cost advantages in the marketplace. Besides winning Galanz a greater market share, a substantial increase in the company's sales could reduce its unit cost through scale economies in production, distribution, and components sourcing, which would make the price cut profitable. But the company needed to make sure that the increased efficiencies would outpace the price cut and increase its total profitability. Galanz believed that it had a chance to do this if it was deliberate and meticulous in planning and executing the price war.

Two months before launching the campaign, Galanz began to run its production lines on a three-shift, 24-hour-a-day schedule so that it had ample inventory to meet the expected surge in demand. Galanz picked August to start the price war because it was the off-peak selling season. Manufacturers generally cut back their production and distribution about that time. Starting a price war at that sleepy time of year would catch their competitors off guard.

In August 1996, Galanz announced a steep price reduction of 40% on some of its key models and an average price reduction of 20.1%. All major Chinese media reported the news of Galanz's opening salvo. Retailers embraced the price war with open arms because it could help them build store traffic and sell more of their other products. In many cases, they were even willing to take lower profit margins, 8% instead of the usual 20%, on Galanz products during the price-war period, to boost traffic even further.

Competitors were caught unprepared and dazed.

In a number of cases, Galanz's price-reduction levels on some products were higher than their own gross profit margins. Most of the small manufacturers did not respond quickly because they believed that Galanz was simply dumping excess inventory in a low selling season. As expected, W–X was also slow on the draw.

The outcome of the first price war could not have been more positive for Galanz. Before the price war, Galanz's gross profit margins were close to 40%. After the price war, sales had increased by about 200%, and the average unit cost shrank approximately 50%. The combined gain in scale and share meant that Galanz's net profits actually *increased* after the price cut. Even for products in which the magnitude of the price cut was bigger than the company's initial profit margin, Galanz still profited because of cost reductions. By the end of 1996, Galanz's market share had increased from 25% to 34.5%.

The huge success of the first price war convinced the executives at Galanz that a deliberate price war was a viable strategy, not only in the short term, but also for the long run. From October 1997 to October 2000, Galanz initiated four more price wars and executed them with increasing sophistication. In each round, Galanz cut its prices substantially—by double-digit percentages (still up to 40% in some cases). The sales increases were also substantial, at 100%–200%. As a result, the company became more and more dominant (see Table 3.1). In each round of price wars, Galanz achieved an average unit cost reduction of about 30%–40%, making the price war essentially "free," even in per-unit terms. Because of those victories, the Chinese media treated Galanz as an ever-victorious army and its executives as conquering generals.

The numbers might look random, but the generals were actually dropping their prices with surgical precision, to inflict the maximum damage on their competitors. Since the first price war, Galanz had adopted a simple and systematic way to set its price to drive volumes. Before the price war, it had always set its price at the break-even point of its nearest competitor. For example, if the second player's annual sales were 2 million units, Galanz would set its price at the break-even level for those 2 million units. During a price war, Galanz would lower its price below the opponent's break-even point, which was still above its own break-even price. Using this strategy, Galanz always kept its strongest rivals reluctant to cut prices, while picking up market share from the weakest fish. The strategy succeeded brilliantly. About 120 microwave oven manufacturers were in the market in 1996. By 2003, the three largest manufacturers dominated more than 90% of the market.

Breaking Out By Breaking Even

Price wars aren't always a winning strategy. Even in China, firms sometimes initiate price wars on impulse and bring ruin on themselves and their industry, just as American marketing textbooks warn. However, these cases demonstrate that price wars can be a potent, effective marketing strategy when deployed with forethought and skill and under the right circumstances.

What constitutes the right circumstances? The calculations that executives at Galanz and Changhong made fit into a simple framework Western executives are familiar with in a different context: incremental break-even analysis (IBEA)—a simple equation used to set prices that also contains almost everything an executive needs to know to plan, execute, and fight a price war.

A price war always starts with a firm initiating a deep price cut in an industry, as Changhong did with color TVs and Galanz did with microwaves. When a firm initiates such a price cut, it expects to benefit from higher volume, either right away or at some point in the future. In the short term, the firm can benefit only if its sales go up sufficiently to offset the lost profit per unit. That's where IBEA comes in handy—it identifies how much sales need to increase to make up for the contribution margin sacrificed by the price cut.

The Galanz case is a good illustration. While planning for the first price war, Galanz reduced its product price by as much as 40%. At the time, the company had a contribution margin (cm) of about 40%, or cm = 40%. The company forecast that the price cut could generate enough volume to achieve unit cost savings (Δc) of 30%–40%, or on average $\Delta c = 35\%$. By plugging all these numbers into the formula, it's clear that if the sales of Galanz's products increased by more than 90.5% as a result of the 40% price cut, its profit would be higher after the price cut than before. Here, $\Delta q = 90.5\%$ is the threshold increase in sales required for Galanz to profit from the 40% price cut. Galanz expected its sales to increase by 100%. Therefore, initiating the price war was the rational thing to do—and looked positively brilliant afterward, when sales actually rose by 200%.

The whole art of price war is implicit in the IBEA. The formula in Figure 3.1 illustrates that it is more tempting for a company to initiate a price war, a deep price cut, if it faces a small Δq, the threshold increase in sales required for a firm to profit from the price cut. With a small Δq, it does not take much sales increase for a company to jump over the hurdle and benefit from a price cut. Therefore, the company should have more incentive to use price as a weapon and to initiate a price war. This means that if we look for industries where Δq is small, we know where a price war is more likely to break out and which firms have the most incentive to initiate it.

$$\Delta q = \frac{\Delta p - (1 - cm)\Delta c}{cm - \Delta p + (1 - cm)\Delta c}$$

Definitions:
Δq Breakeven sales increase in percentage
Δp Magnitude of a price cut
cm Contribution margin in percentage (before the price cut)
Δc Reduction in marginal costs in percentage due to the price cut

Figure 3.1 Incremental break-even analysis

IBEA analysis exposes an important truth about who leads price wars. Although price wars are often thought of as an underdog strategy—the marketing equivalent of the Hail Mary pass—the strategy is actually most effective when the most efficient competitor in a high-margin industry executes it. If the initial profit margin is high, only a small increase in sales is needed for a firm to benefit from a price cut. This explains why the first price wars were color TVs and microwave ovens and why all subsequent price wars in China happened in what were initially high-margin industries such as consumer electronics, home appliances, personal computers, mobile phones, telecommunications equipment, cable TV, and automobiles. It also explains why Chinese companies tend to start price wars when they enter Western markets. With their cost advantages and favorable exchange rate, every business in the West looks like a high-margin business!

The formula also clarifies the role scale plays in price wars. As the reduction in marginal costs (Δc in the formula) gets bigger, the percentage in added sales required to break even (Δq) declines. This means that price wars are more likely to break out in industries with significant scale economies. The industries in China that have been plagued by price wars all have significant scale economies. Even in the West, price wars flare up in industries with significant scale economies, such as PCs, electronics, and airlines.

A larger reduction in marginal costs (Δc) decreases the break-even point (Δq), suggesting that the firm that is more skillful in taking advantage of its scale is most likely to be the one that initiates a price war, all else being equal. Both Changhong and Galanz were firms that consciously and skillfully exploited scale economies to their own benefit. Price wars are also more likely in industries with little product differentiation. In a highly differentiated industry, customers would require a huge incentive to switch from one firm to another, resulting in a higher break-even hurdle in most cases. In China, price wars almost always break out when products in the industry become standardized, leaving little room for further technology innovations and quality improvements.

As a firm must generate enough sales increase to offset the per-unit loss to benefit from a deep price cut, we can further look into the art of price war by examining how a firm can generate the required sales increase. A firm can cross the threshold sales increase in three ways, either through a significant market share increase, a significant increase in the industry demand—or both. Thus, there are a number of things that a firm can do here in planning and executing a price war. First, to the extent that it is easier for a small market share firm to increase its market share, a firm with a small market share may be better positioned to use price as a weapon and to initiate a price war, while a big market share firm may want to think twice. For that reason, we rarely see firms with a dominant market share start a price war.

The timing is also critical. A firm has a better chance to increase its market share if the competition is unable or unwilling to react swiftly. A clumsy, half-hearted response from the competition gives the war-initiating firm the time and space to fill distribution channels and to occupy new sales territories. As discussed earlier, both Changhong and Galanz carefully considered competitive reactions and the most opportune time to fire the first shot.

Third, even if competitors react swiftly by bringing down their own prices, an astute firm can increase its market share if it is prepared. As competing firms lower their prices, the firms that gain market share will be the ones that have products on hand to sell. A firm that has prepared for a price war—by increasing its inventories, ramping up its production, cornering strategic resources, securing distribution channels, or boosting its production capabilities—will be best positioned to increase its market share. Changhong and Galanz both made elaborate preparations in all those activities before they fired their first shot, while competitors were caught napping.

Fourth, a firm can gain a larger market share when less cost-effective firms in an industry are weeded out. A price war strains every firm in an industry. When less efficient firms buckle first, the survivors fatten their market shares. Clearly, this factor was crucial to Changhong and Galanz, who made explicit calculations to consolidate their respective industries and achieved that objective. Looking more broadly, this motivation has repeatedly surfaced as a cause of war. With the relative youth of the Chinese market, its many industries, and wide range in sophistication and operating efficiency, it is not surprising that China has more price wars than the West.

Through many price wars, Chinese executives have also learned that to weed out firms that are not cost-efficient, they do not necessarily need to fight a prolonged, bloody campaign. A "shock and awe" strategy can quickly convince inefficient rivals to get out of the way if they perceive that resistance is either futile or fatal. Both Changhong and Galanz considered this in planning and executing their price wars. This explains why Chinese companies are gung ho about charging a price 30%–50% lower than competition, instead of a gentlemanly 10% or 20% lower, when they invade a market in the West.

However, companies might have a reason to wage a price war even if they can't use it to increase their market share. Another important factor in a firm's price war calculus is the change in aggregate product demand. When a price war breaks out, even if all competing firms in the market are equally efficient and all follow suit by cutting their prices so that no firm can gain any additional market share, firms can still benefit from price wars if the action sufficiently expands the industry demand. In the West, people tend to forget the days when the markets for mundane products such as microwave ovens, color TVs, and refrigerators were growing at a fast pace and the total demand for them was price elastic. In China, consumer goods production is still a high-growth business with high price elasticity: Lower the price for a popular consumer good and you can flood the market with new consumers.

For this reason, in the coming years, as growth levels off, we expect to observe fewer price wars and more focus on nonprice competition—at least in China.

Forward, March

As far as we can detect, there is nothing intrinsically Chinese in the calculus that Chinese executives use to plan and execute their price wars. The fact is, Chinese companies compete in an environment characterized by growing markets, heterogeneous firms with a wide distribution of cost efficiencies, and new technologies with significant scale economies—perfect weather for a price war. Similar circumstances often occur in other emerging-market economies—not just China and, not even necessarily in another of the emerging market giants. A major technological innovation anywhere can lead to huge gaps in an industry's scale economies everywhere. For example, engineers in tiny Estonia built Skype, which began almost as a toy but is now undercutting the market share of regular telephone service and even video conference networks.

Price wars aren't for everyone. In Western markets, oligopolistic competition among equals in mature markets encourages more subtle marketing strategies. However, as with any other strategy, a price war can be useful in particular circumstances. A company can take a rational approach to plan and execute a price war when such opportunities arise.

Defenders should not be discouraged either. Just as winning a price war is not an exclusively Chinese talent, losing a price war is not intrinsically American. High-margin companies faced with the terror of the "China price" can anticipate what might follow and preempt it. Such moves can be quite successful. For example, Philip Morris, perhaps worried that cigarette prices would soon be cut by generic brands and knowing that RJR had low profit margins because of a heavy debt load from its recent leveraged buyout, cut its prices by 20% in April 1993, effectively neutralizing both its new and old competition for the near future.

IBEA suggests two broad principles for fighting a price war. First, as Sun-Tzu put it in his *Art of War*, "the highest realization of warfare is to attack the enemy's plans" so that one can subjugate "the enemy's army without fighting." Translating this to a price strategy, companies should do two things that discourage a competitor from starting and benefiting from a price war: increase the hurdle (Δq) competitors face to discourage them from thinking about price cutting in the first place, and differentiate the product enough to make substitution difficult.

Second, if a price war must be fought, don't just take a defensive posture. Once again, Sun-Tzu put it best: "One who cannot be victorious assumes a defensive posture; one who can be victorious attacks." In the parlance of IBEA, a company should always strive to position itself to profit from rising consumer demand (Δq) or any possible redistribution of market share.

Endnotes

[1]Much of this chapter is adapted from the paper "The Art of Price War: A Perspective from China," by Z. John Zhang and Dongsheng Zhou (2007).

[2]Henderson, David. "What are Price Wars Good For?," *Fortune* (May 1997), 135 (9): 156.

[3]Rao, Akshay R., Mark E. Bergen and Scott Davis (2000), "How to Fight a Price War," *Harvard Business Review* (March/April), 107–120.

[4]Engardio, Pete and Dexter Roberts. "The China Price," *BusinessWeek* (December 6, 2004).

4

Thinking Small

"Many a pickle makes a mickle."
Anonymous

People get annoyed when someone fusses over pennies. Even most of the phrases we have that concern pennies are filled with contempt: penny-pinching, penny-wise and pound-foolish, penny-ante, a penny for your thoughts—almost no one has a good word for the lowly cent. But it would be a mistake to overlook the penny. Some of the most innovative pricing strategies—and biggest business opportunities—of our time are, quite literally, penny-ante plays.

The experience of Muhammad Yunus is a good lesson in the value of pennies. The Bengali development economist won the Nobel Peace Prize in 2006 for an insight he had in 1976. While a lecturer in economics at a university in Bangladesh, the American-educated professor began looking for ways to help his desperately poor country develop. After interviewing 42 poor villagers at length, he found that they could all improve their income substantially if they could borrow the grand sum of $27. After he lent them the money and was paid back, then lent more and was paid back again, he tried to find a bank that would make these kinds of tiny loans on a bigger scale:

> But the bankers still said, "Oh, you're a fool. They will repay the money this time, but the moment you loan more, they'll stop." I was told that the loans were repaid because the borrowers were all from one village where I had been meeting

and talking with the people. So I did it in two villages, then five, 10, 20 villages, 30 villages, 100 villages. Each time it worked. Each time the bankers waited for the whole thing to collapse, and it did not. It grew.[1]

At the time, the idea must have seemed ludicrous to the bankers he spoke with—noble, maybe, but ludicrous. Bankers are used to handling big numbers and dealing with suit-wearing customers. More importantly, conventional banking is founded on collateral. As one of banking's oldest jokes puts it, a banker is a person who lends money to people who don't need it. If the borrower didn't have anything that the lender could hold as security, how could the principal be guaranteed by anything except an exorbitant interest rate?

But Yunus proved them wrong. He had discovered that in a certain context, the poor would repay the money. First, his competitors added some discipline to the market. The local moneylenders he competed with charged anywhere from 10% interest per month to 20% interest *per day*. Second, the small circles of women to whom he lent would vouch for each other's creditworthiness, creating a working alternative to the collateral system. Whether it worked because the groups provided a way to assess credit risk (women, it turned out, were better credit risks) or because the groups created a mechanism for turning their social capital into a kind of nonmonetary collateral based on reputation, Yunus did get repaid.[2]

Nor did Yunus's experience prove unique to Bengali villages. One recent study by the microfinance unit of the World Bank found that charge-offs by Yunus's Grameen Bank and more than 1,000 other microfinance lenders amount to not more than 3%. Although the global downturn has affected performance somewhat, microfinance loans have still performed better than many portfolios. Charge-offs climbed from 1.2% before the economic crisis to 2%–3%—still low compared to most conventional banks.[3] Average return on equity of a microfinance institution was 2.8%.[4] But that's just the average return, and is undoubtedly low in part because it includes the many micro-finance institutions that operate on a nonprofit basis. For the profit-oriented, returns are far higher. Even as most of the big banks lost billions in 2008, Gil Crawford, the CEO of Microvest, a Bethesda, Maryland-based fund manager that holds $70 million in microfinance debt, reported in February 2009 that his fund had returned 20% in 2008. "It's beating our targets," he said.[5]

Today Yunus's Grameen Bank and thousands of other microfi-nance institutions have become a vast and growing industry, at least in terms of customers served. Lending a few dollars at a time, they now reach more than 150 million customers a year, 100 million of them among the poorest of the poor, people who live on less than $1.25 a day. Financial industry analysts project that microfinance institutions will have more than 200 million customers by 2015—and even that is only the beginning. Deutsche Bank, which now invests more than $4 billion in microfinance efforts around the world, projects that although microfinance organizations now have $15 billion to $25 bil-lion in outstanding loans, the worldwide demand for microcredit could be as high as $250 billion.[6]

Deutsche Bank is not alone in its optimism. C. K. Prahalad, a busi-ness professor at the University of Michigan, argues in his influential book *The Fortune at the Bottom of the Pyramid* that the world's four bil-lion poorest people could actually be a source of economic growth. "If we stop thinking of the poor as victims or as a burden and start recog-nizing them as resilient and creative entrepreneurs and value-conscious consumers, a whole new world of opportunity will open up," he writes.[7]

Prahalad argues that Western companies' failure to build more business in the developing world is less a result of the poverty of these four billion people than the poverty of the Western corporate imagi-nation. He writes that simply repackaging goods in different sizes or reimagining a service in such a way that the cost is somehow within reach of the lowest strata of income can uncover a huge underserved market. In India, for example, some consumer goods manufacturers already understand the advantages of micro-sizing. Prahalad says that a huge market is growing of products sold by the single serving, enabling the poor to buy shampoo or soap, for example, when their cash flow permits.[8] Redefining a product in other ways can also create new markets. Iqbal Quadir, founder of a cellular telephone service in Bangladesh, now partly owned by Grameen Bank, discovered that although Bangladesh was too poor for individuals to own cellphones, he could still create a viable cellular network by giving cellphones to women in villages who could run their own pay phone service.[9]

Nor is this simply charity work. All those pennies could create a sizable business opportunity. Prahalad estimates that the four billion poorest people in the world have $13 trillion in purchasing power parity (PPP)—roughly the same size as the GDP of the United States or the European Union measured in PPP.[10] If Prahalad is right—and the successes of millions of entrepreneurs in China and India suggests that he is—some of the biggest business opportunities in history are just waiting for marketers prepared to think small.

Pitching Pennies

But the penny isn't valuable only in terms of marketing to the developing world. It can create significant opportunities in other contexts as well. As marketers have known for 100 years, one penny more or less can make a real difference in sales—and sometimes even create value for the brand.

Consider what happens when the price of a product is set at $9.99. Studies going back nearly 70 years have found that as many as 5% more customers will buy a product priced at $9.99 than when the same product is priced at $10. Marketers believe that many consumers always round down prices to the nearest lower dollar.[11] Interestingly, where that "just below" price is set doesn't seem to matter much. For example, many prices in China end in 88—a number traditionally considered lucky. A student of ours there found that the last digits could be raised to 99 without any impact on sales—and this in an extremely price-sensitive market.

On the other hand, adding a penny can sometimes help build a brand. Some recent research suggests that experience has trained customers to associate round-number prices with quality, maybe because in the past companies that used round numbers tended to be less focused on cost. Now, some companies trying to position their products as high quality set price at a round number.[12]

Just Pennies per Day

Pennies can also be a useful way to reframe an offer. For example, charities have advertised that viewers can help someone "for just pennies a day," even if the aggregate payment is far higher. Retailers have also tried this pitch: One Chicago mattress retailer used to claim that it was possible to sleep on one of its mattresses "for only 10¢ a night."[13] As transparent as it might seem, pennies-a-day reframing actually seems to work. For example, when magazine publishers began reframing their subscription offers in the 1980s as price per issue instead of price per year, their advertisements became 10%–40% more effective.[14]

Why? One scholar believes that pennies-a-day pricing enables us to think of the price as part of a trivial, affordable out-of-pocket expense, such as buying a cup of coffee or a lottery ticket.[15] But the pennies-per-day strategy isn't without its own set of risks: A competitor can also discourage consumers the same way. Reframing the money those pennies per day actually represent as a single lump sum can effectively take it back out of the mental category of trivial expenses.[16]

Many marketers profit from this lack of attentiveness by consumers. The experience of Mobil Corporation before its merger with Exxon is a good example of how a company can find incremental profits simply by taking a closer look at its pricing. In 1995, while searching desperately for more revenue, Mobil decided to conduct some market research to learn why people pull into a particular gas station. Most consumers said they chose stations because of brightness, safety, and convenience. Such factors turned out to be more important than cost for 80% of customers, despite the fact that the gas price may be the most visible price in America. The company's research also suggested that, as aware as Americans are of the price of gas, they were not acutely sensitive to slight price differences. The new strategy of brightening and polishing the stations and charging a premium for being the safer, cleaner rest stop enabled the company to increase revenue as much as 25% at participating stations.[17] Analysts estimated that if this enabled Mobil to charge even a 2¢ premium on each gallon of gas, it could add as much as $118 million to the company's bottom line.[18]

Sometimes a closer look at a penny can even create a new kind of offer. In 2007, the U.S. Postal Service (USPS) decided to try to find a way to help customers avoid the nuisance of having to buy a roll of 1¢ stamps every time the price went up. The USPS released a "forever" stamp ahead of the price increase—a stamp that would be good even after the price rose to 41¢. The stamp proved extremely popular with consumers, who were happy to avoid the need to buy all those 1¢ stamps. It was also profitable for the USPS because the forever stamp amounts to an earlier adoption of its latest price increase. This could add up to a substantial sum because each penny increase is worth as much as $800 million a year, and consumers have an incentive to stock up on forever stamps before a price increase. The forever stamp also reduces costs because the government no longer has to print all those 1¢ stamps in anticipation of a price hike.

Supersize My Profits

As the success of the forever stamp suggests, consumers are often willing to pay a little for a modification to an offer if they feel it's a good deal. In fact, McDonald's built much of its business on this home truth. Although McDonald's discarded its "Supersize" program a few years ago in the wake of bad publicity from the documentary *Super Size Me,* all kinds of restaurants and food outlets still follow its pricing logic by giving customers apparent discounts on larger sizes. Food typically is only one-third of a restaurant's costs, which makes it relatively inexpensive for restaurants to supersize portions—particularly when it's a high-margin product such as Coca-Cola or French fries. For example, the 16-ounce "grande" at Starbucks doesn't take many more coffee beans to produce than a 12-ounce "tall," but the grande costs 11% more—$1.89 compared to $1.70, making the big cup seem like a good deal to the consumer.[20] Similar economics prevail in many kinds of food and beverage outlets.

Credit for the supersize idea goes back to a discovery in the 1960s by David Wallerstein, president of the Chicago movie theater chain Balaban & Katz. Wallerstein was an innovative marketer who, incidentally, also pioneered a number of other beloved American treats, including butter on popcorn and ice in drinks. Frustrated by not being able to boost snack sales despite two-for-one offers, combo deals, and matinee specials, Wallerstein had an epiphany: "People did not want to buy two boxes of popcorn, *no matter what.*" It made them feel piggish. Instead, he would change the unit size so they would have more but feel less self-conscious. He would still sell only one order of popcorn, but he would give them the option to take a bigger box. Customers would feel they were getting a deal with the jumbo size, but because popcorn cost so little to make, the snack would still yield a high margin for the company.[21]

It turned out that Wallerstein's gut instinct was right. People would eat more—and pay more—if the offer was repositioned as a single, larger box. In fact, the plan worked even better than he hoped: Thirsty popcorn buyers bought Coke as well. Not surprisingly, his idea swept the industry—and probably helped catch the eye of McDonald's founder Ray Kroc, who brought him on as one of McDonald's board of directors.

Despite Wallerstein's success, McDonald's was not easily convinced that when it came to portion sizes, bigger would be better business. Kroc wasn't persuaded until the mid-1970s to give the idea a try. However, even after the success of large fries, the company resisted franchisees' call for supersizing other items, fearing that customers would see large sizes as a form of discounting—a move that conventional marketing wisdom suggested would ultimately cheapen the perceived value of the product.[22] Eventually, the more-is-more faction won, and they turned out to be right: More was in fact more profitable. Large fries turned out to be extremely popular.

After seeing McDonald's success, other fast-food restaurants also began living large. So did convenience stores. In the mid-1970s, a midlevel manager of a 7-Eleven named Dennis Potts began experimenting with the Big Gulp, a 32-ounce drink. Since then, the retailer has pushed the frontiers of bigness even further, offering the nearly aquarium-sized Super Big Gulp (42 ounces) and all kinds of other food in bigger portions, from hot dogs to candy bars. "There is nothing magical about it," said Potts. "The customer gets a good value, and the retailer makes more money on a per-sale basis."[23]

More recently, fast-food outlets have begun using software to upsell customers in a different way. A number of software systems are now being integrated into point-of-sale software that generate different value propositions on the fly after customers place their orders, offering them such deals as the opportunity to buy a cookie at half off the regular price instead of getting their change back. On a small cash purchase, the customer likely perceives the "deal" as a kind of double discount—first, because the item is offered at a lower cost, and second, because many customers don't really value their small change as money and instead let it pile up in jars and drawers.

A few years ago, the maker of one of these systems, Digital Deal software, added a video display, giving customers a picture of the offer, which adds 60¢ on average to a $5 check. The computer generates offers on-the-fly, after evaluating customers' choices and the dollar amount. The system can also work with an automated audio voice system for drive-through windows: "We have a deal for you. We can make your total an even [$5.00] and give you [a medium French fries] or [a medium milkshake]. Which would you like?"

The software takes advantage of another penny-focused behavioral quirk as well. If the coin change is less than 20¢, the offer is set to round up to the next higher dollar. The system's vendor, Retail DNA, claims to have found that if the customer is given more than a 25% discount, they are just as willing to accept "over the dollar" as "under the dollar" offers.

The company estimates that as many as 35%–50% of customers accept their "deal"—a number that translates into 3%–5% more sales. The software is designed to use rules and parameters that ensure a minimum gross profit of 50% and customer savings that range from 25% to 75% but average 40% (offers are randomized to avoid training customers to anticipate a particular "deal" and changing their order accordingly). During a year, all those quarters can add up. Retail DNA claims that a quick-service restaurant that generates $1.2 million in sales can increase sales by 4.2%, or $50,000, and increase pretax profits by $16,000.[24]

Hey, Big Spender

Casinos have also learned the value of reframing wagers in penny terms. Despite all the stories about the high rollers who are wined and dined in casinos to get them to put more money on the tables, small gamblers are also important customers, if not the most important customers for some casinos. And not only small, but the smallest of all: someone who bets pennies.

A penny-ante gambler might not sound like anyone a casino would be interested in, but the casinos began to install more penny slot machines after market research showed that penny slot players stayed longer and didn't necessarily lose less money than players gambling in higher denominations. In 2005, one Australian machine company claimed that its penny machines brought in an average of $400 a day—double the take of an ordinary machine.

Penny-ante thinking has all but revolutionized many casinos in recent years. The new penny machines have worked so well that Connecticut's Mohegan Sun casino[25] went from having a few hundred low-denomination machines on the floor in 2003 to more than 2,000 in 2007.[26]

Casinos seem to be switching to the lower denominations for two reasons. First, they're increasingly popular. Part of the reason is that the new video machines, in which bets are mostly made using cash cards, not coins or tokens, provide more entertainment value. Customers can either gamble longer or play multiple games at the same time—sometimes up to 100 different games at once. Although few customers bet the maximum, even fewer bet the minimum. Many people seem to like the action of playing so many games at one time.

Casinos also like the penny machines because the new computerized machines are frequently more profitable. An Indiana gambling commission noted that the percentage "hold"—retained cash—on penny slots is higher than dollar slots. The most profitable $1 slot machine in Indiana retained 8.2% for the casino, compared to 11.9% for the top penny machine. That 8.2% is actually high by industry standards, but the 11.9% take on the penny machines is reportedly about average.[27] In Las Vegas, the $1 machines pay out 96%–98%, compared to around 90% for the penny machines.[28]

A number of theories have been proposed to explain why gamblers don't realize that penny machines are "tighter" than higher-denomination machines. One is that the minimum price of entry is lower, so customers perceive them to be less risky. Multiple lines also seem to offer more chances to win than a single pull on a $1 or a $5 machine.[29] Finally, because multiple-play games produce more payouts at once, they give customers the perception that they are winning more often than is actually the case.

Information technology is also creating opportunities for casinos to bring in not just pennies, but even fractions of pennies. Mohegan has even installed half-penny machines—a division that is possible now that players play slots with value cards instead of coins. Gas stations also push the outer limits of price tolerance by selling gas to the 9/10ths of a penny—which some authorities have estimated amounts to an extra $1.3 billion in profit every year in the U.S. market alone.

Breaking down the price into units so small that the consumer no longer cares about them can also overcome consumer resistance to adopt a new product. Skype for example has grown into the world's largest voice-over Internet protocol (VOIP) telephone service, partly because of a penny-focused pricing strategy. Unlike other VOIP providers who needed to convince clients to bet $20–$30 a month on subscription to an unfamiliar technology, Skype gave customers a way to experiment with VOIP without forcing them to choose between VOIP service and conventional telephone service. The upshot: Skype now has a global user base of 330 million, even as its key competitor, Vonage, which chose to grow using a more traditional subscription model, remains stuck at 2 million.[30]

As the dotcom boom proved, "nearly free" works as a long-term business model only if it is supported by something genuinely profitable. In the case of Skype, the fact that the cost of routing calls over the Internet is nearly zero pulled the cost of that transmission near zero and helped give the eBay unit the edge it needed to undercut its competitors and become the Internet's dominant telecom service. Co-founder Niklas Zennstrom explains the company's ambition this way: "We want to make as little money as possible per user."[31]

Even the market for intellectual property can sometimes be expanded by reframing the serving size. For more than 50 years, until 2002 or 2003, most music was sold in units of 12 songs, first on the long-playing vinyl album and later, the compact disc. However, the rise of file sharing began to force a change in that practice ten years ago, when college students began to swap digitized versions of songs.

At first, the industry fought the shift. Even those who embraced the idea of change spent a lot of time arguing about the right model for selling music in the digital age. Some held that a subscription model made the most sense. Others argued that the price didn't matter all that much because the music itself would become a loss-leader for other products, such as live concerts or memorabilia.

As we saw with Radiohead's "pay as you wish" model in Chapter 1, that debate continues today. Apple seems to have hit on what will likely be the dominant music sales model for some time to come, by selling the album in single-song units. Apple's music download site, the iTunes Store, offers consumers a compelling proposition for music based on price. Instead of paying $10 or $20 for a CD of 10 or 12 songs, consumers pay 99¢ for a single song. They buy only the songs they want and then download them to their iPod, computer, or other MP3 player.

Although a number of elements have created value in Apple's iTunes music scheme—the gathering of vast music libraries on a single platform; the company's digital rights-management solution, which convinced music library owners that they would not lose control of their property; and the iPod itself, which offered a fundamentally more convenient way for consumers to store and listen to music—the value of changing the "serving size" from the album to the song should not be underestimated. Since its opening in 2003, the online iTunes Store has grown into the largest music vendor in the United States. By January 2008, Apple Computer announced that consumers had downloaded more than five billion songs from its iTunes Store. Globally, iTunes is a huge force as well, dominating more than 70% of the world's online music sales.[32]

Micropayments are turning out to be useful in other circumstances as well. For example, they are making it possible to charge for certain kinds of virtual goods in multiplayer games, creating an economy that could scarcely exist otherwise. Although multiplayer games have been around since the early days of the Internet, some game-platform developers have begun adding features in recent years to encourage the creation of a kind of economic life within that "world"—a feature that seems particularly suited to games such as Second Life, which are more forums for a kind of online social interaction than games in the traditional sense. In Second Life, two kinds of money-making opportunities have evolved within this virtual world where "residents" interact and play out their life fantasies, and both deserve recognition as innovative micropayment strategies.

The first is issuing play money within the game—Linden dollars, in the case of Second Life. Or rather, apparently play money: Linden dollars aren't quite Monopoly money. The company actually makes money exchanging Linden dollars with real-world money. Linden Labs, the developer of Second Life, buys and sells the scrip, making money in either direction when the money is transferred in or out of the game, at an exchange rate of 270 Linden dollars to the U.S. dollar. Although users can buy currency only in L$1,000 bundles, they can make payments down to L$1—about one-third of a cent. That might not sound like much, but Linden Labs reports that transactions worth up to $1.5 million occur every day—about $3 per visitor.[33] If you want to have a good life in the virtual world and do the things you want to do, you need to have Linden dollars to foot the bill.

As all those transactions suggest, the circulation of Linden dollars is making others money as well, besides Linden Labs. As Linden dollars have a transferable value guaranteed by the company, real entrepreneurs have found genuine money-making opportunities inside the virtual world. Some of these have apparently occurred by chance, as the virtual products of a fantasy career catch the eye of other players. For example, a New York supermarket manager spends part of his leisure time running a fashion boutique in Second Life, in a shop he bought from Linden Labs two years ago ($230 for a 375m² plot of virtual land). Buying imaginary land might not seem like a promising investment, but it seems to have worked for the owner, Peter Lokke. Today Lokke claims to earn nearly $300 a day—in real dollars—from sales of his clothing designs, which other players put on their avatars (the figures the user controls on the screen).

Part of what makes Second Life commerce profitable for Lokke and others is that they have nearly no cost of doing business beyond what they pay Linden Labs for their un-real estate. "My supply is limitless," Lokke says. "There's no bottom line. The costs are only what I pay Linden Labs."[34] As we have seen with other Internet-related products, this lack of a marginal cost means the price of a good can almost reach zero yet still remain profitable after the first-copy cost is paid.

A few people have built even bigger volume-oriented businesses in Second Life. Ailen Graef, a Chinese teacher living in Germany, became Second Life's first millionaire in 2006. Having first parlayed a $10 investment into a $1 million portfolio in virtual property, Graef has since built a business of 80 full-time employees who "build" what would be 40km of gated virtual communities for Second Lifers if Second Life were the first life. "I am like Wal-Mart," Graef says. "The margins are small, but the volume isn't."[35]

The experiences of Graef and Lokke are unusual but not unique. On average, more than 165 residents earn $5,000 or more in any given month. This might not seem like much considering that Second Life is a "place" with a daily population of around 500,000, except when you consider how few needs a person can actually satisfy online. And it may eventually prove to be an interesting opportunity for the poor but Net savvy: The $200 or more earned by roughly 4,000 Second Lifers every month is within striking distance of the average wage of the urban Chinese worker.

It's also early days for such new "worlds." Some analysts predict that in four or five years, the vast majority of Internet users will spend part of their time on "Metaverse" sites, creating vast new markets for all kinds of virtual services and products. These kinds of forecasts are notoriously difficult to get right—they end up either going too far or stopping too short—but it seems certain that whether the game analysts are right or not, micropayments will become a growing part of the way at least some people work, play, and transact business online.

A Small Price to Pay

But penny-wise thinking isn't just for selling songs or virtual dresses. In the past four decades, marketers have effectively multiplied demand for condominiums, yachts, and even private jets by simply adjusting the "serving size."[36]

The fractional ownership or time-sharing idea goes back to the 1960s, when a resort owner in the French Alps pitched a new concept to European skiers: "Don't rent a room; buy the hotel—it's cheaper!"[37] The idea spread to Florida during the oil crisis of the early 1970s, a time when American consumers were pinching pennies and developers stuck with unwanted condominiums were struggling to dispose of money-sucking inventory.

For the consumer, the pitch looked enticing: a second home at a fraction of the cost. Instead of buying an entire vacation home or condominium, consumers would pay for only the one or two weeks a year that they would use. When developers pitched their product this way, many consumers perceived it to be a good value: no maintenance headaches, plus they'd pay only for the time they were at the resort. At the same time, all those "pennies" add up for the company, which makes more money selling all those shares than it ever would by selling a single condominium.

For the developer, it's an even better deal because it broadens the market for the asset. Suppose a developer is selling a $60,000 summer house. One person can spend $35,000 for a summer house, and the other person can spend $45,000, but neither can afford the house. However, if they pool their resources, the two can spend $30,000 and $40,000, and their total budget rises to $70,000. If they buy at

$70,000, the developer earns $10,000 more than his original price, and the two owners get a house neither would have been able to afford alone for less than they might have paid. Everybody wins. In addition, the developer can sell many more and better quality houses by aggregating the fractional demands.

Today the average cost of a two-bedroom time share is roughly $18,000, not counting annual maintenance fees of roughly $500 and various other charges. For the prospective purchaser, that price appears low compared to a vacation home, which could cost 10–20 times that much (and appears even lower because 70% of the buyers choose to finance 60%–90% of the purchase through convenient in-house financed mortgages).[38]

Time shares have also created more supply in a different way: The growth of time-share networks has encouraged demand shifting in ways that create more stable year-round demand.

Not surprisingly, the time share business continues to grow at double digits every year, as it has for more than a decade. More than four million Americans now own time shares in more than 1,600 resorts. Industry polls suggest that time share owners are happy with their purchases, especially now that most time-share schemes are more akin to memberships in "vacation clubs," networks of time-share resorts all over the country that are also exchangeable for stays in other resorts all over the world.

Nor are time shares just a product targeted to the middle class. Today luxury apartments and multimillion-dollar ski chalets are also being sold by the slice. Although the value proposition is a little different—more of the products sold at the top end of the market are true deeds of title and not, as in the mass-market product, a "pre-purchased vacation"—the lure of the bargain remains the same.

Yachts, luxury cars, and other symbols of the good life are also being sold in shares, with perhaps somewhat more limited success. Even designer sunglasses, jewelry, and handbags are being conveyed to consumers on what amounts to a fractional basis. Bag Borrow or

Steal (bagborrowsteal.com) is a mail-order company that enables women who want high-fashion accessories, such as Louis Vuitton purses that could cost thousands of dollars, to instead rent them by the week for a few hundred dollars—giving fashionistas the look they want right now without tying up a month's rent in a designer bag.

The appeal of fractions isn't limited to consumers. Businesses have also been enticed by fractional schemes. Fractional jet ownership for example, has grown into a huge business since the founding of the first fractional jet company, NetJets, in 1987. Richard Santulli, a businessman tired of cooling his heels at airports, thought of a way to expand the market for private jets. Although few people or companies would or could pay the millions it took to buy a whole private jet, he believed many people would buy a share in one.

Convinced of the logic, the former Goldman Sachs partner bought a charter company and transformed it into the world's first fractional jet company.[39]

Beyond the consumer appeal of planes-by-the-slice, Santulli found cost efficiencies on the supply side in pooled airline ownership that were not all that different from the efficiencies of a time share as opposed to a second home or a hotel. Corporate jets were underutilized assets that flew, on average, only 250 hours a year, compared to 2,500–3,500 hours a year for a major carrier's airline. Combining the fractional demand boosted usage to 1,000 hours a year, which helped dramatically reduce the cost of the fractional ownership.[40]

Today, approximately $400,000 will buy a 1/16th share of one of NetJets' fleet, equivalent to 50 hours of flying time, instead of the more than $6 million it takes to run a jet full-time—a price that works out to not that much more than flying first class. It is even possible to buy a smaller share: Through a subcontractor, NetJets also sells 1/32nd shares, or 25 hours of flying time.

As with time shares, lowering the price of entry created a much larger market—NetJets alone (which controls about half the market) flew 600 aircraft in 2006, making 350,000 flights worldwide to nearly 3,000 airports.[41]

But fractional ownership is not without its risks. The biggest risk is the temptation to oversell the number of shares. Fractional jet owners at some companies, for example, have become disgruntled in the past few years because the airplanes in which they have shares have logged so many air miles that they are depreciating at a more rapid rate than initially scheduled, reducing the value of their investment. Too many ongoing maintenance costs can also lead to disillusionment by undermining the initial value proposition of fractional ownership as a low-cost, hassle-free way to fly your "own" jet. Finally, capacity can be an issue as well, if someone doesn't work out the math early on. However, a well-designed network with properly set volume can overcome all these problems: Santulli, a mathematics PhD, figured out early on that, given enough planes, he could promise a jet to every customer with just three hours' notice and almost no chance of running short of capacity.

Of course, whether you're selling shares of jets or bags of popcorn, success requires making sure that the sum is worth more than the parts. This is as true for private jets as for French fries. If there isn't a gain in value on the side of the seller—and, ultimately, the customer—the strategy won't work.

Many companies lose their way because they haven't understood the minutiae of their cost structure and let profit leak out in a variety of ways. Often, for example, companies design sales incentives in ways that move the most units without considering their underlying profitability. Wharton marketing professor Len Lodish once noted a famous snack food company that compensated its sales force not on the profitability of sales of its chips and cookies, but per pound sold—essentially, encouraging sales teams to focus on its heavier, lower-margin products. Too often companies redesign their products in ways that encourage sales without concern for underlying profitability. One consultant, for example, tells the story of a marketing manager whose line of sales at Costco was expanding by 7% a year went from "hero to goat" in an instant after company executives learned that the cost of the product redesigns responsible for the gains had been raising the cost of the product by 6% every year—essentially wiping out the profitability of the gain in volume.[42]

Mind-Forg'd Manacles

Traditionally, most businesses have succeeded by appealing to a select group and then charging that group as much as possible. But in today's global market, the best way to grow big may be to think small. As Prahalad has suggested, the greatest challenge of business today is how to charge the least and serve the most. Many Indian retailers for example, work to find ways not to keep prices up, but to follow the Skype model of looking for ways to keep their costs as low as they possibly can so they can create the widest possible market for their products.

All over the world, marketers have begun to understand the somewhat counterintuitive idea that a company charging an infinitely small price can still make a lot of money when it serves an infinitely large number of customers. In this new context, the gains from each sale don't have to be obvious. By definition, they might not be obvious because the most successful penny strategies typically require some basic reinvention of the value proposition—questioning, as Tata Motors has in creating its revolutionary new $2000 Nano, about what constitutes an automobile, or as Yunus did, when he asked why the poor could not be good loan customers.

The challenge seems to be more about the limits of perception than opportunity—escaping what the poet William Blake called "mind-forg'd manacles," which prevent people from reimagining their products and their pricing in ways that could reach millions or even billions more customers than they ever dreamed possible. As

Yunus says, "My greatest challenge has been to change the mindset of people. Mindsets play strange tricks on us. We see things the way our minds have instructed our eyes to see."

Endnotes

[1]Globalenvision.org, "The End of Poverty: An Interview with Muhammad Yunus" (August 23, 2003).

[2]Counts, Alex, *Small Loans, Big Dreams: How Nobel Prize Winner Muhammad Yunus and Microfinance Are Changing the World* (New York: John Wiley, 2008).

[3]"Sub-Par but Not Subprime: Microfinance," *The Economist* (21 March 2009).

[4]Engen, John, "Is Microfinance Ready for Its Next Big Leap?" *U.S. Banker* (February 2009): 18.

[5]Ibid.

[6]Deutsche Bank Research, "Microfinance: An Emerging Investment Opportunity (19 December 2007).

[7]Prahalad, C.K., *The Fortune at the Bottom of the Pyramid* (New Jersey: Prentice Hall, 2004), 2.

[8]Ibid., 17.

[9]Knowledge@Wharton, "Building Sustainable Startups in the Developing World" (14 January 2005).

[10]Prahalad, 30.

[11]Stiving, Mark, "Price-Endings When Prices Signal Quality," Ohio State University, Management Science (December 2000).

[12]Ibid.

[13]Gourville, John T., "Pennies-A-Day: The Effect of Temporal Reframing on Trans-action Evaluations," *Journal of Consumer Research* (March 1998): 395.

[14]Ibid.

[15]Ibid.

[16]Ibid.

[17]Sullivan, Allana, "Mobil Bets Drivers Pick Cappuccino over Low Prices," *Wall Street Journal* (30 January 2005): B1.

[18]"A New Vision at Mobil," *National Petroleum News* (June 1995): 62.

[20]"Will Diners Still Swallow This?" *New York Times* (25 March 2007): 1.

[21]David Wallerstein obituary, *New York Times* (January 6, 1993).

[22]Critser, Greg, *Fat Land: How Americans Became the Fattest People in the World* (New York: Houghton Mifflin, 2004), 21.

[23]Ibid.

[24]www.retaildna.com.

[25]Hamner, Susanna, "Heaven from Pennies," *Business 2.0* (August 2005).

[26]Peters, Mark, "Coins Dropped from Slots: Casino Phases Out Token-Operated Machines, Switches to Paper," *Hartford Courant* (May 1, 2007).

[27]"Slot Players Beware: Pennies Can Add Up," *Chicago Sun Times* (March 2, 2008).

[28]Cooper, Marc, "Hey, Big Spinner ...," *Los Angeles Times* (April 15, 2007).

[29]Ryan, Joseph, "Illinois Casinos Beat the Odds," *Daily Herald* (July 20, 2008): http://www.dailyherald.com/story/print/?id=221651.

[30]"Vonage Growth, Losses Set New Lows," *Telecomweb* news break (August 7, 2008).

[31]"The Skype Hyper," *The Economist* (October 6, 2007).

[32]Jobs, Steve, Keynote address at Macworld (September 2008).

[33]Emily Rotberg, "Tiny Sums Now Changing Hands," *Financial Times* (January 30, 2008); and September 2008 Second Life Economic Statistics, http://secondlife.com/whatis/economy_stats.php.

[34]Bennett, Jessica and Beith, Malcolm, "Alternate Universe: Second Life Is Emerging As a Powerful New Medium for Social Interactions of All Sorts, from Romance to Making Money," *Newsweek* (July 30, 2007).

[35]"Going Gets Real in Virtual World," *Gulf News* (March 29, 2008): http://www.zawya.com/printstory.cfm?storyid=GN_29032008_10201339&l=000000080329.

[36]Emling, Shelley, "Buying a Share of Luxury on the Sea," *International Herald Tribune* (April 6, 2007): 17.

[37]Bowen, David A., "Timeshare Ownership: Regulation and Common Sense," *Loyola Consumer Law Review* (2006): 1.

[38]Murphy, H. Lee, "No Time Out for Timeshares," *National Real Estate Investor* (August 8, 2008); and Upchurch, Randall, et al., *Timeshare Resort Operations* (Oxford: Elsevier Butterworth-Heinemann, 2004).

[39]Kroeger, Fritz, *Beating the Global Consolidation Endgame* (New York: McGraw Hill Professional, 2008), 157.

[40]Martin, Nathan A., *Flight to Financial Freedom—Fasten your Finances* (SOM Publishing, 2007), 85.

[41]Kelly, Emma, "NetJets—Poised for Growth," *Airport Business* (March 2007).

[42]Knowledge@Wharton, "The Challenge of Customization" (June 16, 2004).

5

The Automatic Markdown

"[R]etail prices are finally determined by the incomes of the masses of buyers...this is the dominating power in fixing prices."
Edward A. Filene, 1927, founder of Filene's Basement

Everyone knows clothing stores mark up their prices, often by a lot. Clothes are usually priced from 100% to as much as 500% above wholesale. Stores typically offer their customers occasional reprieves throughout the year by running some products on sale, but in every case, the customer is at the mercy of the merchant. By design, shoppers can never know when a product they like will be on sale. Their only choice is either to pay the price they see on the day they are shopping or to move on. And the more in-demand the item is, the more money shoppers will need to shell out. It's the nature of the industry.

The most common countermove to this dominant pricing strategy is to take a value focus, such as Old Navy's strategy of pushing private-label clothing. Although this can be a profitable business as well, the downside is that it gives up any chance to extract even a portion of the fashion premium. But stores can use other ways to discount besides "pile it high and let it fly." Syms, a New York–headquartered apparel retailer, has developed a method that captures the fashion premium even as it discounts goods that aren't moving. Syms uses an ingenious automatic markdown system that simultaneously encourages immediate purchases and return visits, keeping sales velocity high and steady. At Syms, each price tag for women's dresses gives customers several pieces of information they can use to help make their buying decisions: the nationally advertised price, the "Syms price," the price that is set on the day that the dress first reaches the floor, and three prices, each lower than the prior one, which are triggered at ten-day intervals thereafter. The price for an item is marked down automatically on pre-specified dates so that customers interested in a particular dress know precisely when it will be on sale—the exact opposite of the normal practice in high-end retail.

Why does Syms do this? Certainly, in an ordinary store, a loyal clerk won't tell the customer whether a specific item is going on sale the following week. Tipping off the customer would be against the interests of the store and probably grounds for dismissal (Not that any clerk would do it—why would she want to give up a chunk of her commission?). The whole point of not being transparent is to keep that fashion premium high for as long as possible, then discount it only when it reaches the kind of invisible expiration date that marks many fashion-driven products.

An Automatic Markdown Rundown

As good as the traditional pricing system works—and retail clothing would be much poorer if it didn't work—it does miss some gaps, which the Syms automatic markdowns fill very well. We count at least six important advantages of the Syms system, compared to conventional fashion pricing.

First, the big price tags help anchor the initial price by contrasting the Syms price with the national retail price. It is always difficult for consumers to judge the intrinsic value of a dress, especially if they like it and have plenty of money in their purses. If consumers see that the price of a dress was originally advertised elsewhere at $249 but find it on sale at Syms for only $209, they will likely perceive that the dress is already on sale. This initial price helps frame the value of the dress in consumers' minds and becomes an important part of the purchasing decision.

Second, knowing the price is declining adds time pressure to the purchase decision. It's no secret that fashion-driven items are constantly declining in price because every moment is nearer to the time when they will no longer be fashionable. Syms takes advantage of the fact that consumers know the game. For Syms shoppers, transparency about when the prices will be marked down actually adds more psychological pressure by creating a greater perception of scarcity. In an ordinary store, shoppers might decide to go home and think about whether to make a purchase, confident that the same suit or dress will still be on the rack in the near future and maybe even marked down at some point. Retailers know this and try to counteract this tendency. Some try to undermine consumer complacency in a number of ways, such as putting only one size of a particular outfit on a rack or introducing a number of variations in what is essentially the same garment. But a store using an automatic markdown system applies an additional source of pressure. As consumers know that a scheduled sale is on the way and that the sale will make the piece of clothing more desirable to more buyers, they may decide they don't want to take the risk of waiting, especially if they like the piece and are emotionally attached to it. Automatic markdowns can generate a sense of urgency shoppers might otherwise lack.

This seems to work especially well for items whose perceived value is volatile or has a high degree of time value. Syms automatic markdown sales are only for its women's dresses, which the Syms 2007 annual report notes (perhaps with a bit of understatement) "are susceptible to considerable style fluctuation."[1] Although the automatic markdown is a Syms trademark, the women's clothing segment is the only segment in which the markdown is used—and represents less than one-third of the store's total sales.[2]

Third, automatic markdowns enable Syms to reach customers who have varying degrees of price sensitivity. Syms automatic markdowns make it possible to serve both fashion-oriented and value-oriented customers at the same time—a clever workaround of one of the biggest problems of pricing fashionable clothing: how to serve a market in which fashion trends, personal taste, and wide ranges of price sensitivity can make it extremely difficult to choose the optimal price. By using automatic markdowns, Syms can charge a high price to customers who are not price sensitive, who can afford to pay more and don't want to wait to take a dress home, while still offering a low price to customers who are more price sensitive, who do not mind waiting, and who are tolerant of having fewer choices.

Fourth, automatic markdowns can help add some excitement to the routine of shopping. Handled right, automatic markdowns seem to make shopping fun for some. Customers interviewed about Filene's Basement, Syms' forebear in automatic markdowns (which we discuss in the next section), often talk about the experience as "gambling" or "a game"—and recall either the joy of finding a bargain or the suspenseful wait on a purchase until the next scheduled price drop. Other aspects of the automatic markdown systems also seem akin to gambling: the pleasure of getting something for nothing, the chance to participate in a game with seemingly inviolable fixed rules (publicly posted rules seem to have always played an important role at Syms and, in the past, at Filene's Basement), a competition in which strangers are pitted against one another for something of value, and finally, a special situation where ordinary inhibitions don't apply. Many stories about Filene's talk about the degree of class mixing in class-stratified Boston for example and the fact that some women continued to change in the aisles even after changing rooms were installed in 1992.

Fifth, automatic markdowns boost repeat traffic. They are a good way to entice shoppers to visit a store repeatedly, particularly for price-conscious shoppers who might otherwise avoid stepping into a store at all. Price-conscious customers who come back intending to look for something they saw the week before may well walk out with something different. Creating such a habit is extremely useful: Marketers have long known that the more time customers spend in a store, the greater the likelihood they will succumb to an impulse purchase. Whether or not they find their bargain this trip, chances are good that they will find something else the next—and even when the chances are low, they are certainly much better than if they hadn't returned to the store at all.

Sixth, the transparency of the discounting reduces buyers' remorse as well. Knowing the price at which an item lists at a full-service department store, the price Syms lists right now, and the prices Syms will offer in the future if the item stays on the rack enables customers to make purchasing decisions that leave them with less buyer's remorse yet keeps their faith in the value of the designer label still unshaken. Finally, the automatic aspect of the system reduces the need for retagging, which is typically an enormous source of expense. Some experts have found that adjusting prices in a drug store—a retail format not dissimilar to a clothing store such as Syms because it has multiple products and multiple suppliers—can amount to as much as 0.59% of a store's total revenues, or roughly 50¢ per item, per price change.[3]

Setting the Automatic Sale in Motion

An automatic pricing system seems to work best with certain kinds of products. First, the product should have some time value, such as fashionable clothing or seasonal products (think of Christmas ornaments in January). A second important quality is that customers must be emotionally involved in their purchases and have a strong sense that they know the normal price so that they can appreciate a bargain. The Syms tagline "An Educated Customer Is Our Best Customer" has it exactly right: Whatever their level of income, the best Syms buyers will be those who know fashion and place value on brand names but are aware that such clothes are highly marked up. Fashion-conscious customers are also more likely to be impatient and will have a strong preference for buying now while certain trendy items are still hot, instead of waiting until they are more affordable but "over." Finally, the product on sale must be perceived as somewhat unique. If a customer perceives a product to be unique, she is more likely to feel the urgency to make the purchase now. For that reason, Syms is smart not to use the pricing mechanism to sell men's suits or children's clothing.

Syms' Automatic Ancestor

Although Syms is the only major U.S. clothing outlet that currently uses automatic markdowns, it was not the first. That honor probably goes to a retailer we mentioned in passing earlier in this chapter, a Boston discount clothing shop that opened in 1909 as the Tunnel Bargain Basement and billed itself as "a new kind of store!"

For once, the advertisements didn't exaggerate: Filene's Basement, as it came to be known, was a new kind of store. Unlike other retailers—including Filene's Department Store—that marked down merchandise on a more haphazard basis, Edward A. Filene's basement store featured not just discount clothes, but clothes discounted on a new kind of pricing method: the automatic markdown. Prices were marked down automatically by 25% after they had been on the shelf for 12 days. Six days later, they were cut again, to 50% of the original price. And another six days after that, they fell to 75% of the original price. Six days more on the rack, and the item would be given to charity.

Conventional retailers reportedly scoffed at the new store and called it "Filene's Folly."[4] They bet that customers would simply wait for goods to hit bottom. But it turned out that Filene understood human nature better than his critics. The store proved wildly successful with the public, although it reportedly did not generate a profit in its first ten years. Surprisingly, the pricing model itself seems to have been a key to the store's success, as indicated by the fact that by 1919 the store had been renamed "the Automatic Bargain Basement." By 1930, the "ABB," as Bostonians had begun to call it, pulled in one-third of the store's total revenue—a fact that delighted Filene, an extremely progressive retailer who introduced a number of innovative concepts to retailing besides the automatic markdown system, including the 40-hour work week and a minimum wage for women.[5]

Filene's Basement was a beloved institution in Boston for most of the twentieth century. Through two wars, three recessions, and a depression, Bostonians stayed loyal to the store. Hem lengths rose and fell, and styles changed and changed again, but through it all, the automatic markdown system was always in fashion. The markdown process was so successful in generating business that only 0.05% of inventory ever needed to be given to charity. By 1950, the Basement was selling 500,000 dresses a year, 90% of them before the first scheduled markdown.[6]

At the heart of Filene's business model was a profound insight into pricing that many retailers still have not understood, even today. As one of his associates later explained, "He had begun to conceive of a store as a place in which to sell goods, not as a place in which to carry goods which did not sell."[7]

Instead of setting price merely by adding a margin on top of cost, Filene later told a group of fellow retailers that price was actually best understood as a function of what the buyer could pay. He estimated that roughly 85% of the sales of any given product could be "determined roughly by the income of the customers served, ranging from those of lesser means to those of ampler means."[8] Filene argued that companies needed to pay more attention to setting prices that matched the income of their customers. "The businessman of the future, whether manufacturer or merchant, will make more money by reducing prices than the businessman of the past ever made by raising them," he predicted.[9] Filene clearly understood that everybody loves a bargain!

The store continued to capture the hearts of many Bostonians and visitors to Boston into the 1980s and 1990s. A 1982 *New York Times* story even described Filene's Basement as "a major Boston tourist attraction, an obligatory stop on the circuit including nearby Faneuil Hall and the Quincy Market redevelopment."[10] It's been described as the "second most sacred secular space in Boston," right behind Fenway Park, a democratic space "where you leave your status at the door" and join with your fellow shoppers, united in a common passion for bargains.[11]

Although the original Filene's Basement is closed, possibly just for renovation or perhaps for good, most newspaper stories about the store still mention the store's unique pricing method—a sign that, for most shoppers, the pricing method itself continues to be an important part of the Basement's brand equity. "The automatic markdown game turned the stress of holiday shopping into a 'winner takes all' entertainment," one shopper recalled when the store closed at the end of 2007.[12] Nor was she the only lamenting shopper: A "support group" for bereft Basement customers even organized itself on Craig's List, www.craig.org.

But although the two institutions are obviously related, Syms represents a step forward in pricing method evolution. Syms offers the automatic discount only on selected clothing, particularly dresses—an important distinction because men's suits, for example, do not date as quickly. If men's clothing were put on automatic markdowns, you could count on most men to wait until the lowest price. By contrast, Filene's offered the same stair-step discounts on everything, which perhaps led to unnecessary discounting. The discounting itself is a bit different, too. Syms marks down its goods over a longer window of time, with a less rigid formula, which probably acts to conserve the value of the product a bit longer. This variation enables Syms to generate more precise information over time so that it can fine-tune its initial price and the magnitudes of its markdowns.

Few Takers

Despite the success that Syms and Filene's Basement have had with automatic markdowns, automatic pricing has made surprisingly few converts over the years. Wanamaker's, a Philadelphia department store, tried its own version in 1984 without much luck. Even the Filene's Basement branches that opened outside Boston in the late 1970s ultimately stopped using the store's unique pricing structure.[13]

Few businesses other than clothing retailers have experienced success with the pricing method either, or even tried it. Those rare successes show that automatic markdowns do have tremendous potential. Harris Rosen, an independent, Orlando, Florida, hotelier, built up Florida's largest independent hotel company thanks, in part, to a clever adaptation of the Filene strategy.

An independent thinker similar to Filene (Rosen has been described as "the Frank Sinatra of hotel magnates—he does things his way."[14]), Rosen thrived, in part, thanks to his willingness to adopt innovative pricing strategies. But Rosen's creativity had a different motivation than Filene: necessity. Filene was a scion of a department store magnate for whom the Basement was a kind of pet project, maybe even an experiment motivated partly by what we would call today a social responsibility agenda. However, Rosen innovated out of a simple quest for professional survival. After losing two jobs in a row, first with Hilton and then Disney, the headstrong Rosen decided the only way he could succeed would be to go into business for himself. He scraped together enough for a down payment and bought an Orlando hotel in 1974, just in time for the OPEC oil embargo. The event killed Florida tourism and threatened to take Rosen under right along with it, almost before he started. "There is nothing more depressing than owning a business without any business.... It's awful, it's depressing, it's scary," Rosen recalled in a talk at Cornell University in 2007.[15]

Instead of simply hoping that business would improve before he defaulted, Rosen hustled. His first experiment was a "pay as you wish" strategy. Rosen asked long-distance coach-tour operators in New Bedford, Massachusetts, where many coach-tour companies were based, what they would be willing to pay to stay in his "virtually empty" 256-room hotel:

> I had little business cards and I would ask the owners of these motor coach companies, tough, tough old Yankees, what rate they would be willing to pay if they stayed at my hotel in 1974. The rates ranged from $7 to $9 a night. Eagerly, enthusiastically, I signed these little contracts by putting my initial next to the rate....[16]

The gambit worked. By the end of the year, Rosen had generated a $150,000 profit—even as most of his competitors were still struggling.

Rosen's second innovation was the automatic markdown of hotel rooms. Building upon his insight during the 1973–74 recession that an empty room was a total loss, Rosen developed a way to reduce the room price as the day wore on and the likelihood grew that the room would stay vacant. With the Rosen system, the longer the rooms remained unrented, the more the price fell. A one-night stay that might have been rented at full price in the morning might go to half-price late in the day. This policy has worked equally well in good times and bad and kept Rosen's occupancy rate above 90% most years, even during years when most of his competitors' occupancy rates hovered around 80%. Rosen has sometimes likened the system to the yield-management systems that airlines and cruise liners use. But because the price is posted and the amount by which prices are marked down is publicly known, we see it as more similar to Filene's old pricing policy.[17]

Now that hard times are hitting consumers again, some merchants seem to be giving automatic markdowns a second look. In Braintree, Massachusetts, outside Boston, Bin Ends opened in May 2008 as a discount wine and spirits merchant with an automatic markdown model. Bin Ends, which claims to be the first off-price retailer of fine wines and spirits in the United States, has consciously modeled itself on Filene's and Syms. Bin ends, in wine-industry jargon, are overstocks, closeouts, and inventory reduction. At Bin Ends, stock is marked down every three weeks, first by 25%, then 35%, and then 45%.[18] Bin Ends also has an online store, and the retailer promises prospective customers the ability to conduct "treasure hunt–style shopping from the comfort of their own homes."[19]

Fresh & Easy, a new U.S. grocery chain owned by Tesco, the U.K. retailer, is also experimenting with automatic markdowns as a way to dispose of about-to-expire items. However, one industry critic doesn't think the model will work well for food. "Either the product won't sell because consumers will fear it is too old, not fresh, and maybe dangerous. Or it will sell, in which case consumers won't buy the full-priced items," writes Jim Prevor, a perishable food industry writer.[20] We're not so sure. Customers do not act en bloc. At least two conditions conducive to automatic markdown pricing are also present at Fresh & Easy. First, different consumers have different degrees of willingness to pay for the products Fresh & Easy sells, but the retailer does not know who is willing to pay what. Second, as with women's dresses, the value of the products on sale at Fresh & Easy decrease over time. However, not all the conditions are in place: The inventory of the goods on sale is not limited.

Although critics of the automatic markdown system object to it on the grounds that it causes the retailer to undersell, the contrary proposition is closer to the truth: An automatic markdown system can actually teach a retailer a lot about where to set a price. Regular, stepped markdowns make it relatively easy to track the particular point in time and point along the discount line where demand starts to falter— knowledge that the retailer can use next season. For example, Syms tracks all its sales data, and analyzing this data helps it optimize the initial price of the next new shipments.[21] Simply tracking sales data using the automatic pricing method Filene developed nearly 100 years ago should, at least theoretically, optimize prices nearly as well as some of today's seven-figure price-optimization software.

Going, Going...

The reason we can say with some confidence that an automatic markdown system optimizes returns is that it is essentially a kind of a slow-motion Dutch auction, which some economists have found can generate higher returns than other forms of auctions in certain circumstances.

Dutch auctions run from high price to low price—the opposite direction from the low-to-high English style of auction, in which bidding starts at the bottom and the good being purchased eventually goes to the highest bidder. In a Dutch auction (so-called because a Dutch cauliflower farmer invented it in the 1870s as a way to simplify his sales process), an initial high price is given, and the auctioneer keeps lowering the price until the goods find a bidder.[22] Like the Syms buyer, Dutch-auction bidders do not have to buy now, but by holding off, they face the risk that someone else will bid first and walk away with the prize—a near certainty because the price will keep get cheaper.

In addition to some of its classic applications, such as wholesale flower auctions in the Netherlands, Dutch auctions are now in use on eBay as a way to sell multiple items, and by the Federal Bank of New York, which sometimes uses the auction method as a way to sell U.S. Treasury bonds.[23] High-tech companies also have experimented with Dutch auctions, and U.S. and European governments have used Dutch auctions to sell bandwidth. For example, Google sold its $2.7 billion initial public offering (IPO) in 2004 via shares purchased on a Dutch auction.

California investment bank WR Hambrecht + Co. is credited with popularizing the use of the Dutch auction as a way to conduct an IPO. Founder Bill Hambrecht argued that the Dutch auction is a better way to set IPO prices than the standard English auction because it removes a perverse incentive of investment banks to set initial offering prices lower than the expected trading price. In the case of a popular company, he argued that a lower price gave a big profit to the bank and its most favored customers—a practice that was good for the bank and good for the clients who benefit from access to the issue, but not so good for the client trying to raise cash on its equity.

Traditional English auction–style IPOs prevent real price discovery from taking place, Hambrecht argued, because most early buyers take a quick profit and flip it to investors who are more eager to own the stock for the long term. "In a Dutch-auction system, there is really no guaranteed profit, because you're pricing it very close to the full demand in the marketplace," Hambrecht said.[24] (Of course, that's assuming that the auctioneer names the right top price and allocates all the shares to the winners. In spite of the precaution of allocating shares by Dutch auction, Google's bankers somehow managed to do alright. Google shares had an opening day "pop" of 18%, less than the 20%–30% some tech companies gained in the dot-com days, but certainly a healthy return on a one-day investment.[25])

Nor do the applications for Dutch auctions end there. People continue to discover new ways to use the method. The owner of a mansion in Auckland, New Zealand, recently tried to sell his property via a Dutch auction instead of listing a price, and did fairly well with the method. Bids started at $5 million New Zealand dollars and closed at $2.65 million ($1.48 million U.S. dollars). According to a local appraiser, the auction resulted in a purchase $300,000 above market value in New Zealand dollars.[26] Other real estate sellers might find this method interesting especially in these volatile times, particularly because it works well as a way to sell unique products—which may be one reason the U.S. Treasury Department proposed selling $700 billion in "toxic" debt via a Dutch auction in fall 2008.[27]

Although a seminal 1961 paper by Columbia University professor William Vickrey showed theoretically that the four basic auction types—English (conventional), Dutch, sealed bids, and Vickrey auction (a variation of the sealed bid in which the winner pays the second-highest price)—more recent researchers have found that, in practice, auction performances actually varies in certain circumstances. In the late 1990s, not long after Vickrey won the 1996 Nobel Prize in Economics for his auction work, some researchers found that Dutch auctions sometimes yield less than conventional or sealed-bid auctions. More surprisingly, others discovered that on some online auction sites, Dutch auctions actually yielded 30% more proceeds than a conventional English-style auction.[28]

To reconcile this wide and peculiar gap between theory and practice, two economists at Pennsylvania State University, Elena Katok and Anthony Kwasnica, tried designing different types of auctions. In the English-style test auctions, fast- and slow-speed auctions yielded similar outcomes. But in the Dutch auction, a fast Dutch auction brought in lower returns than a sealed-bid auction, and slower Dutch auctions tended to yield more than the sealed bid.[29]

These researchers theorize that part of the reason for the differential performance is that bidders lose patience. Bidders decide either that the trouble (in economic terms, the transaction costs) involved in waiting for another round of bidding (or, in the case of Syms, returning to the store) is not worth the difference in cost or that the goods themselves will be worth less if they put off their bids until later. This insight, the researchers speculate, may lead bidders to bid more than they might have if the goods had been sold in a fast, conventional auction.[30] Now you know why Syms still loves its automatic markdown system.

Why All Retailers Don't Go Dutch

As the Dutch auction examples suggest, automatic markdowns won't work for every business. As alluded to earlier, one of the basic conditions for an automatic markdown to succeed is a perception of scarcity. In the women's clothing example, scarcity is reinforced because the latest women's clothes grow less valuable in the course of a season in a way that men's and children's clothes do not. This is probably why the best products to sell via this kind of slow Dutch auction or automatic markdown are unique products; it is difficult in advance to know how much a particular customer will value a particular good. This may be one reason that stores bigger than Syms and Filene's Basement have not adopted automatic markdowns: The larger the store is, the harder it is to create the same perception of scarcity. Similarly, the value of uniqueness in driving interest in an auction helps explain why Dutch auctions are popular on eBay, the Internet's unique-product mecca.

High retail traffic is the other way to promote a perception of scarcity. As with an English auction, the threat of being outbid may help drive the bidder's behavior. Certainly, this seems to be true for Filene's Basement. Retail Ventures, owner of Filene's Basement since 2000, reportedly ended the markdown system in the satellite stores years ago because the program was profitable only in the flagship store, where 15,000 people prowled for bargains every day.[31]

One interesting question is whether the automatic markdown has become outmoded now that pricing software is becoming ever-more sophisticated and capable of helping retailers decide when price points need adjustment. State-of-the-art data mining can calculate not just the best price for a given product, but also how that price will affect the sales of other products—for example, how dropping the price of beer might lead to an overall gain if it boosts the sales of higher-margin taco chips. Some vendors claim that using such a system even in service industries can lead to an opportunity to raise 80% of prices by 1%–3%[32]—a huge jump, given that Accenture estimates that a 1% growth in margin for most companies can lead to a 10% improvement in the bottom line.[33]

The Once and Future Price Tag

However, as with any kind of software, such programs are not a magic bullet. One survey of 18 major retailers found that only half said they could quantify the results of the insights gained using the pricing systems. Interestingly, the kind of products for which this $3 million to $5 million price-optimization software appears to be most successful is precisely the same kind that Syms sells: products with a limited shelf life. "If the life cycle of product is 10 to 16 weeks, that is the sweet spot," says Antony Karabus, founder and chief executive officer of Karabus Management, a Toronto-based retail consulting firm that installs markdown-optimization software.[34]

If that's the case, it might be hard to top the simple markdown method Filene invented a century ago. No other pricing system can, on one ticket, frame a high perceived value for a product, encourage customers to buy right away, and give price-sensitive shoppers a reason to come back next week. It even does a terrific job with price discovery, making it easy to see the exact price point at which a buyer will buy. As Syms, Rosen, and the Bin Ends team have all found, automatic markdowns can be a viable strategy for many kinds of products—and an extremely cost-effective one compared to the present multimillion-dollar costs of installing, operating, and maintaining markdown-optimization software. Customers are also often happy and excited by those automatic markdown price tags—even when in truth their bargain isn't really much of a bargain.

For all these reasons, the history of automatic price markdowns suggests that innovative pricing strategy can be used not only to help improve sales, but even to transform a business. Thanks to the power of his deceptively simple pricing system, Syms created a solid niche for himself in New York and the mid-Atlantic in the same five decades that perhaps a dozen iconic, full-service department stores—from Gimbel's, to Altman's, to Wanamaker's, and others—were acquired or went out of business. Similarly, Filene's use of automatic markdowns helped grow the store into an enduring brand that in time even overshadowed its parent, Filene's Department Store, and every other clothing store in Boston. Over the past 100 years, companies spent billions building and creating brands, but few succeeded nearly as well as these two innovative retailers working with just a few explanatory signs and some date-stamped price tags.

Endnotes

[1]Syms Corp., "2007 Annual Report" (March 2008).

[2]*Plunket's Retail Industry Almanac* (2009).

[3]Shantanu Dutta, Mark Bergen, Daniel Levy, and Robert Venable., "Menu Costs, Posted Prices, and Multiproduct Retailers," *Journal of Money, Credit, and Banking* (November 1999): 685. The 39¢ estimate stated in the article has been updated to reflect 2007–08 dollars using the inflation conversion estimates of Robert Sahr, Oregon State University (http://oregonstate.edu/cla/polisci/faculty-research/sahr/sahr.htm).

[4]Berkeley, George E., *The Filenes* (Wellesley, Mass.: Branden Books, 1998). 123.

[5]Ibid.

[6]Ibid.

[7]Filene, Edward Albert and Mittell, Sherman Faian l, *Speaking of Change: a selection of speeches and articles* (Freeport, NY: Ayer, 1971 (reprint)).

[8]Filene, Edward, "What Is Happening to Retailers, Wholesalers, and Producers—the Way Out," Interstate Merchants Council Convention (Chicago, February 1, 1927).

[9]Berkeley, *The Filenes.*

[10]Blumenthal, Deborah, "Boston's Favorite Bargain Store," *New York Times* (April 18, 1982): http://www.nytimes.com/1982/04/18/travel/shopper-s-world-boston-s-favorite-bargain-store.html.

[11]Mendez, Teresa, "Backstory: the Original Bargain Basement," *Christian Science Monitor* (February 22, 2006): http://www.csmonitor.com/2006/0222/p20s01-ussc.html.

[12]Jenn Abelson, "No Holiday Twinkle Here," *Boston Globe* (November 21, 2007): http://www.boston.com/business/globe/articles/2007/11/21/no_holiday_twinkle_here/

[13]Ibid.

[14]Maxwell, Scott, "The 25 Most Important People in Central Florida," *Orlando Sentinel* (December 27, 2007): B1.

[15]Harris Rosen talk, Cornell University (2007).

[16]Ibid.

[17]McDowell, Edwin, "His Goal: No Room at the Inns," *New York Times* (November 23, 1995).

[18]Goodison, Donna, "Wine dealer aims at close-out market," *Boston Herald* (April 29, 2008).

[19]"Bin Ends Opens," *PR Newswire* (July 15, 2008).

[20]Jim Prevor's Perishable Pundit blog (February 12, 2008).

[21]*Plunket's Retail Industry Almanac* (New York: Plunkett Research) 2009.

[22]Kambil, Ajit and van Heck, E., *Making Markets: How Firms Can Design and Profit from Online Auctions* (Cambridge: Harvard Business Press), 2002.

[23]http://pages.ebay.com/help/buy/buyer-multiple.html.

[24]Interview with Bill Hambrecht, *Frontline*, PBS (August 2001).

[25]Robinson, Sara,, "For Google Investors, a Crash Course in the Mathematics of Bidding," *Society for Industrial and Applied Mathematics News* (October 26, 2004); www.siam.org/news/news.php?id=258.

[26]"Bidding at Dutch Auction Reaps Reward for Buyer," *New Zealand Herald* (December 11, 2008).

[27]Moyer, Liz, "Bailout Auction Far from a Sure Thing," *Forbes* (September 9, 2008).

[28]Carare, Octavian and Rothkopf, Michael, "Slow Dutch Auctions," *Management Science* (March 1, 2005): 365-373.

[29]Katok, Elena and Kwasnica, Anthony, "Time is Money: The Effect of Clock Speed on Seller's Revenue in Dutch Auctions," SSRN-id673527 (2003).

[30]Carare, Octavianand Rothkopf, Michael, "Slow Dutch Auctions," *Rutcor Research Report* (2001).

[31]Moin, David, "Filene Expands i3Group," *Women's Wear Daily* (September 12, 2006).

[32]Bergstein, Brian, "Pricing Software Could reshape retail," Associated Press, San Francisco Chronicle, April 29, 2007, http://www.zilliant.com/downloads/Forbes_042707_Pricing_Software_Could_Reshape_Retail.pdf.

[33]Lager, Marshall, "The Price is Right...You Hope," *CRM Magazine* (October 1, 2008) 33.

[34]Moin, David, "Automating Markdowns: The Keys to Success," *Women's Wear Daily* (January 12, 2007), 14.

6

Name Your Own Price

"The price tag is obsolete."
Jay Walker, founder of Priceline

On June 1, 1998, less than two months after its launch, Priceline.com was "already one of the hottest consumer sites on the Internet," according to a 1998 *BusinessWeek* article.[1] In the following 13 months, more than two million people reportedly bought something through Priceline. *The Industry Standard*, a popular trade magazine of the time, described it as "a whole new way of doing business on the Internet."[2] Excitement climbed so high that *Forbes* even asked in a headline whether founder Jay Walker was "An Edison for a New Age."[3]

Millions of consumers were thrilled. What excited them was not that they could buy airplane tickets online—even in 1998, consumers had plenty of online outlets for airplane tickets, Priceline's primary inventory—but the way they could buy them. Instead of selling the tickets at a fixed price, the site invited consumers to "name [their] own price," to bid however little they liked for a flight they wanted.

The system was simple. First, the consumer looked up a flight. He could specify the date and the destination but not the time of day or the route (which, as we shall see, is a crucial distinction). Then he made a bid. A little while later, he received an email reply. If his bid was accepted, his credit card had already been charged. If his bid had not been accepted, the game was over: He couldn't enter a second, slightly higher bid for the same flight to discover Priceline's lowest acceptable price. Win or lose, the entire process took about 15 minutes.[4] A Priceline.com sales document explained that the system "literally hang[s] buyer money on a 'clothesline' for sellers to see. Attached to the money is a note describing what the seller is agreeing to in order to take the money down off the clothesline."[5] This wasn't exactly true, as the explanation implies some sort of negotiation. In fact, the carriers had already set their reserve prices. Unlike pay-as-you-wish pricing, carriers could refuse the customer's bid. As a consumer's guide to Priceline[6] written a few years later bluntly put it, "'Name Your Own Price' is a lie. The reality is more like 'Guess Our Price.'" This subtle difference sets the two pricing mechanisms widely apart.

Like many other businesses of the dotcom boom, things went swimmingly over the next year or so for Jay Walker, Priceline, and Walker Digital, the "business incubator" in Connecticut where Walker and 25 employees cooked up new business ideas. With its clever online auction model and wacky commercials starring William Shatner, the actor who played Captain Kirk on *Star Trek*, Priceline caught the imagination of investors even more than consumers. The company's stock reached a dizzy $162.37 a share just a few months after it went public in 1999. At its height, Walker was one of the richest men in the world, holding shares worth more than $10 billion. Other investors included Microsoft founder Paul Allen, investor George Soros, cable tycoon John Malone, and Saudi Prince Alwaleed bin Talal.[7] Priceline itself was valued at $24 billion, more than double the value of any of the U.S. airlines for which it acted as a middle man.[8] And Walker touted the Priceline method as not just an innovation, but "the first new pricing system in probably 500 years."[9]

In many interviews, Walker tended to imply that Priceline was ushering in a brave new world of dynamic pricing, a world in which the value of retail goods fluctuated constantly, the way they already do in the airline industry. The picture was perhaps fairly flattering to

Priceline's customers: It's perhaps more pleasant to think of oneself as a kind of savvy commodity trader than as a bargain hunter. It also appealed to investors, who were infatuated at the time with the idea of new kinds of markets. Thanks to his clever positioning, Priceline was seen by the public, particularly the investing public, not as a travel liquidation house, but as the leader of a sort of revolutionary pricing vanguard.

With hopes pumped so high, it's not altogether surprising that the moment didn't last. Extensions into food, cars, and mortgages didn't work out so well. Cash dwindled. Investors became concerned Priceline couldn't live up to expectations. In 2000, the stock dropped almost as sharply as it had climbed, finally hitting bottom at $1.12 on December 26, 2000.[10] Some senior executives fled. Even Shatner, who had been paid in what looked now like worthless stock options, beamed up.

As with Webvan, Pets.com, or Urban Fetch, the innovative e-commerce retailer seemed almost certain to become just one more casualty of the dotcom bust. Then in early 2001, something unexpected happened: The company didn't die. Instead of becoming just one more "dot bomb," Priceline cut back sharply on its marketing expenses and, by the second quarter of 2001, began to turn a profit.

Ten years after its founding, Shatner is back touting Priceline. Investors value the company at $6.77 billion today (as of September 9, 2009). And although it's true that Priceline hasn't taken over the world as the company once predicted, the Norwalk, Connecticut, company has grown into an incredibly profitable business. Priceline generates more than $1.6 billion in revenue and $600 million in profit every year.[11] Each of the company's 1,324 employees generates $1.9 million in revenue—more, on a per-employee basis, than eBay ($608,915 per employee) and Amazon ($945,971) combined.[12]

Why did Priceline live when so many other dotcoms never saw 2001? It wasn't thanks to Captain Kirk. And it wasn't because Priceline sold anything unique. In 2000, as now, plenty of sites sold plane tickets, hotel rooms, and rental cars. Even today, larger rivals such as

Expedia, Cendant, and Sabre control 93% of the online market.[13] To top it off, buying with Priceline involved a lot of drawbacks. Critics found the site clumsy and complicated. To make matters worse, the goods themselves were opaque: The airline, the departure time, and the route were all hidden. Who would go to all that trouble?

Why Priceline Survived

Ironically, the critics had it wrong: Those inconveniences are the reason Priceline survived. Forbes may not have been quite on the mark in christening him the Edison of the Internet Age, but it's looking now as if Jay Walker may well be its Edward Filene. Similar to the automatic markdown system in Filene's Basement, Priceline created a new kind of sales channel that resonated with a certain group of buyers—and, just as importantly, a certain group of sellers. Far from being an oversight, the inconveniences were actually an important part of Walker's business model. It actually acted as a screening mechanism which ensured that only a certain group of travelers would line up for deals.

Walker talked a lot about Priceline being a kind of revolution for consumers, but in some respects, it was more revolutionary for the seller. Priceline enabled transportation and hospitality companies to fill more of their capacity without weakening their ability to charge top dollar to their regular customers. "We shield the sellers' brands so that they can continue to capture more of the market below their own retail prices," explained Walker in one unusually clear January 2000 interview.[14] Some experts believed that the potential for this kind of selling was high. One marketing scholar estimated that, in some industries, profits could be improved by as much as one-third through the use of Priceline-like techniques.[15]

Disguising the brand and other characteristics of the product, which the pay-as-you-wish pricing mechanism does not do, made it difficult for customers to do head-to-head comparison shopping, helping to preserve the premium the seller could charge for its branded product in the same way the tightly packed racks and lack of changing rooms in Filene's Basement protected the full-price sales of Filene's Department Store upstairs. Priceline's opaque sales proposition acted as a new kind of screening mechanism that would cull only a certain kind of customer: bargain hunters for whom price is such an important consideration that they are willing to put up with the risk of paying up front without knowing some important details about the offer.

Those drawbacks, plus the additional hoop of requiring the consumer to make a blind, sealed bid guaranteed by a credit card, created what economists call a "costly signal" that allowed Priceline's client hospitality and travel companies to identify and reach price-sensitive customers they could not target as easily as before. Our colleague Peter Fader described Priceline's core customers as "the niche group of price-sensitive consumers who doggedly clip out supermarket coupons week after week."[16]

And the bidding process itself? It might have felt daring, but economist Hal Varian of the University of California at Berkeley (and the chief economist at Google) derided the Priceline process as "the same sort of mindless activity as clipping coupons—busywork designed to separate the sheep from the goats."[17]

Annoying maybe, but still innovative. The Priceline system might not have been quite as big a revolution as Walker claimed—nothing but electricity or movable type would measure up to that standard—but it did solve an important problem: how to sell to price-sensitive customers without ruining the opportunity to charge full price to non-price-sensitive customers. As with the automatic markdown system in Filene's Basement, Priceline's model created a new kind of sales channel that resonated with a certain group of buyers—and, just as important, a certain group of sellers. The always colorful Walker put it this way:

We discovered the cure for a terrible disease, a disease that
has existed for hundreds of years. Sellers always have inventory that they could sell at a lower price. And there are
always more buyers willing to buy at the lower price, but the
seller can't afford to reduce price without destroying his rate
card. We figured out how the seller can have his cake and eat
it, too.[18]

As Walker said, determining how to charge consumers with different degrees of price sensitivity different prices is one of retail's
perennial challenges. For most products, consumers typically have
different amounts they will pay for any given product. As we have
seen in other chapters, it's usually not easy to offer a range of prices
without jeopardizing the "shelf price" that the least price-sensitive
customers are willing to pay.

Typically, retailers choose one of several tactics to reach price-sensitive customers, all of them somewhat costly. One is to run a sale that
temporarily cuts prices for a specified time period or occasion. Supermarkets and department stores frequently use this mechanism to
deliver low prices to price-sensitive customers who tend to be better
informed about prices and who can wait patiently for a special price.[19]
Rebates are another way to collect price-sensitive demand: Anyone
willing to go to the trouble of filling out complicated rebate forms
must be price-sensitive. Of course, customers are most price-sensitive
at the checkout counter. If they forget to fill out the rebate forms or do
not want to bother afterward, rebate issuers are more than happy to
rake in the full price and keep the "leakage."[20] Sometimes sellers
release slightly differentiated products. Often companies add more
features to a product for the high-end market or disable features for
the low end. For instance, a tech manufacturer might sell silicon chips
that have some of their capabilities shut off. Airlines sell tickets with
more strings attached, such as 14-day advanced purchases or Saturday
night stays.[21] Where a product is sold is another way in which sellers
price-discriminate. Price-insensitive customers would not go out of
their way to shop at Wal-Mart. Alternative sales channels—factory

outlets and surplus discounters—are another physical way in which sellers try to reach the full range of the demand curve.

But perhaps the most popular way of collecting price-sensitive demand is an old American pricing innovation: the coupon. The Coca-Cola Company offered its first coupon in 1894, when Asa Candler, the Atlanta druggist who owned the formula for Coca-Cola, gave away handwritten tickets for a free glass of his new drink. The following year, C.W. Post, the cereal entrepreneur, offered consumers a coupon that gave them a cent off his new cereal, Grape Nuts.[22] Coupon use, always counter-cyclical, first became big business during the Depression and peaked in a downturn six decades later, in 1992—significantly, perhaps, just four years before the Internet took off as a commercial entity.[23] Even now, however, U.S. consumer product manufacturers issue more than 300 billion coupons each year, two-thirds of which are grocery coupons. More than 85% of those coupons are given away through free-standing inserts, the coupon flyers that are often distributed through the Sunday newspapers. If consumers redeemed all these coupons, the total cost would reach $190 billion. However, the vast majority go unused. Redemption rates of 1%–2% reduce the total cash outlay to about $3 billion.[24]

Despite all that waste, consumer goods companies continue to send out coupons by the billion. The reason is that although coupons can be used to encourage trials and measure customer response to advertising, they're most important to companies as a means of price discrimination. "Coupons can serve as a price discrimination device to provide a lower price to a particular segment of customers," says Chakravarthi Narasimhan, a prominent marketing scholar.[25]

Keeping these price-sensitive consumers as customers adds to the company's revenue, albeit at a lower margin. Coupons also support the market share and the higher shelf price of the branded product. The fact that coupon-clipping customers haven't turned to a lower-priced substitute helps the company maintain the ability to keep charging a high price to its non-price-sensitive customers.

However, coupons have some obvious drawbacks. The biggest is the complexity and inefficiency of the coupon supply chain. First, the coupon needs to reach the right customer, most commonly through the Sunday newspaper. This costs about $10 per thousand.[25] Then the retailer must collect the coupons and frequently must be paid to do so by the manufacturer. Finally, the retailer must send the coupons to a clearinghouse, generally located in Mexico to take advantage of lower labor costs. After the coupons are counted, the clearinghouse sends the retailer the total face value of the collected coupons, plus an incentive payment, to the retailer and bills the manufacturer who sponsored the coupon for all the expenses.

Each of these steps adds waste. Manufacturers, clearinghouse companies, and retailers often fight over whether the retailer deserves reimbursement. Coupons are susceptible to fraud, through such scams as "gang-cutting," clipping huge bundles of coupons from inserts and sending them in for redemption, either by using fake store names or through real stores that are in on the game.[27] Sometimes such frauds can be quite substantial: In one recent case, prosecutors allege that a clearinghouse bilked manufacturers out of $250 million.[28]

With Priceline, Walker found a way to get around all those problems for hospitality and transportation companies, two industries in dire need of a more efficient customer collection system. Even now, for the hotels, car rental companies, and airlines, unused capacity continues to be a huge worry. Although advances in yield-management technology and algorithms have helped hospitality and transportation companies reduce their excess capacity, filling every seat and bed at a profitable price remains a distant goal. Among U.S. airlines alone, 500,000 seats go empty every day, according to the most commonly cited figure. Another figure suggests that in the U.S. 20.4% of all seats go unfilled; worldwide, the figure is nearly 25%. Given that the entire airline industry is operating at a razor-thin margin of 0.9% profit, all those unfilled seats represent a huge potential for growth. Indeed, unfilled seats and beds still represent a vast source of potential profit.

The Opaque Sale

Another important benefit of the Priceline system is the fact that, unlike traditional coupons, brand names could be disguised. Of course, opaque sales are not unique to Priceline (although some scholars believe that the one-on-one nature of the Internet is especially conducive to opaque sale propositions[29]). In conventional retailing, an opaque sale is often made by marketing a store brand alongside a branded product. The private-label good is cheaper than the branded version of the same good, giving price-sensitive customers a cheaper alternative. Many consumer packaged goods companies actually act as contractors to grocery chains, essentially serving as the manufacturer for their own competition. For the manufacturer (in the short run, at least), selling a private-label product is clearly positive because consumers do not necessarily know about the product's true identity when they purchase the "opaque" product. The margins between the private label and their own brands are often not very different because the manufacturer typically doesn't need to pay slotting fees to the retailer or invest in marketing. Also, by supplying private-label brands, consumer packaged goods companies gain the flexibility of charging price-sensitive customers a lower price, while charging a high price to non-price-sensitive customers through the branded product. Like coupons, private label popularity rises in hard times. In the U.S., private-label goods represent 22% of all food sales by volume, and the share is growing. In 2008, for example, sales of private-label groceries and consumer products jumped 10%, from $75 billion in 2007 to $82.9 billion, even as sales of branded products rose just 2.8%.[30] In certain segments, the growth is even faster. German value supermarket chain Aldi, which is now expanding quickly in the U.S., sells 95% private label goods.[31]

Of course, opaque sales are not without risks to the brand owner. Early critics of Priceline charged that, in the long run, Priceline's opaque sales method essentially "trained the consumer to be disloyal,"[32] in the words of one marketing professor, who argued that customers trained to make buying decisions without looking at or thinking about the brand name are probably less likely to stick to one brand. Other marketing scholars also believed that opaque buying on Priceline not only eroded some of the brand value for those customers right away, but gave customers a new, lower anchor price for the product. Some anecdotal studies suggest that Priceline users began to think of the price at which they purchased the previously opaque product as the "real" price. Once accustomed, say, to spending a night in a Holiday Inn for $30, some Priceline customers would begin to think of that special offer as the anchor price and not feel comfortable paying anything higher in the future.

Another related risk, at least to the producer of a product being sold in an opaque channel, arises if consumers in both price-sensitive and non-price-sensitive groups decide that the opaque goods are basically the same as the labeled goods. For instance, a carton of Tropicana orange juice purchased through Priceline could easily be compared to the carton of Tropicana purchased directly from a neighborhood supermarket. In that event, the seller company would not have any incentive to cooperate unless Priceline could succeed in segmenting price-sensitive and non-price-sensitive customers. Priceline tries to maintain these boundaries by setting up complex hoops for price-sensitive consumers to jump through. However, there is a limit to how much even price-sensitive consumers are willing to endure for a deal on lower-priced items. Perhaps not surprisingly, Priceline failed to extend the "name your price" model to the sales of groceries and gasoline. "You think about all the other things you could be doing instead of being on the Internet for 45 minutes," said one Greenwich, Connecticut, mother[33] about her experience with the now-discontinued grocery service.

Indeed, as a demand-collection system, Priceline does not seem to work very well in a market where consumers' willingness to pay does not diverge much between price segments. Unlike airline travel, for instance, for which business travelers may be willing to pay triple or quadruple what most leisure travelers will pay, there appears to be a more limited differential in consumer price sensitivity for most smaller-ticket purchases, such as groceries at a store. In that market, consumers already self-select their preferred price level by store: Value shoppers head to the budget chains, upscale shoppers to high-end retailers. Inside the store, however, not many stay obsessed with price information. One study found that 60% of consumers don't even look at the price of a product as they put it in a shopping cart, and 56% of the time, consumers can't guess the price of a product within 5% of the actual price.[34] In this kind of market environment, the consumer's perceived benefit of "naming your own price" is likely to be limited.

Name Your Own Customer

Ten years after Priceline burst on the scene, Walker turns out to have been both right and wrong, like most technology prophets. He was wrong that Priceline would change everything. The truth is that Priceline serves a particular niche market, not everyone for everything. On the other hand, he was right that the technology that powered Priceline would lead to a revolution in pricing.

With the advantage of hindsight, we can see that information technologies drastically expanded the possibilities in pricing, from the point of view of both buyer and seller. These technologies enabled Priceline not only to facilitate customers naming their own prices, but also to usher in some other game-changing pricing practices.

Companies need demand-screening mechanisms such as Priceline only when they don't have a clear understanding of the customers they might be dealing with. Ironically, the same technologies that enabled Priceline to accept bids on the fly also reduce the need for large-scale demand collection. New data collection and data mining systems allow companies to collect, store, and process customer information on a large scale, enabling them to identify potential customers and generate unique offers much more rapidly than was once the case. In a nutshell, the digital revolution has gone beyond enabling customers to name their own price; to an extent, it has also enabled sellers to name their own customer.

These days, many companies do not just set a fixed price and wait for willing customers to bite. They mine databases to piece together a clear picture of a large number of individual customers and actively pursue the most desirable customers with a personalized offer in terms of both product and price. Targeted pricing has gained an unprecedented following in many industries. For a long time now, catalog retailers have sent different catalogs to different ZIP codes, with the prices changed to reflect the demographic. Today vast databases and stronger analytics make it possible to do the same thing, but on a much more granular level: by family, by buyer, and even by buyer on a particular occasion. Knowledge of the customer is now so much deeper, and the speed with which his buying propensities can be analyzed is so much faster, that many new opportunities for price discrimination have arisen.

Although the concept of targeted pricing itself is nothing new—any time a discount is given to a new magazine subscriber or an incentive offered to a customer of a rival firm, the seller is practicing targeted pricing—technology and hypercompetition have changed its nature in recent years. Retailers can now consider long-term loyalties and any other quantifiable differences between customers when they set their prices. By using the increasingly rich and deep range of customer data that can now be gathered and crunched at a reasonable price, retailers are finding new ways to calibrate individual offers based on who the individual is and where their price sensitivities may lie.

This is new. Traditionally, most economists saw only three possibilities for price discrimination. In 1920, English economist Arthur C. Pigou[35] outlined these basic choices. First, he wrote, a firm could charge a different price for each unit sale at the maximum willingness to pay for the unit. It might also reduce its unit price based on the volume purchased, such as offering a discount for bulk purchases. Or it might charge a different fixed price to different sets of customers, such as students or senior citizens.

Most microeconomic textbooks today still use Pigou's definitions. However, the possibilities for price discrimination have evolved far beyond Pigou's three basic strategies. For instance, when Amazon.com targets its loyal customers with a high price for a book while giving a new, occasional purchaser a low price for the same book, it is practicing a form of price discrimination much more complex than Pigou's traditional classifications. It's not exactly what he called the third degree of price discrimination, in which a particular class of customers is charged a particular price based on demographics. Nor is it the second degree because frequent buyers and occasional buyers are both buying the same amount. Nor is it the first kind because the price is not set on the basis of any individual's demonstrated willingness to pay.

However, despite the fact that it doesn't fit Pigou's neat definitions, this kind of advanced targeted pricing has made inroads not just at online retail sites such as Amazon.com, but also in brick-and-mortar stores. At Tesco, for instance, a major grocery retailer in the United Kingdom, advances in customer data collection and interpretation have made it possible for the store to target its customers in ways that were previously impossible except at maybe a tiny rural store or a high-end boutique.

Using profiles developed by information collected through loyalty cards, Tesco learns a variety of facts about what—and when—its customers buy.[36] By leveraging the 40-plus-terabyte database it has collected on the 13 million U.K. families who shop at a Tesco store every week, Tesco and its suppliers use the data to look for trends and opportunities in the market and to target new products; for example, they might discover which price-sensitive customers would be interested in a new mild cheddar cheese. Tesco's Clubcard operation also uses this data to send personalized coupons and other offers to every Clubcard household every quarter, a huge operation that accounts for more than 6% of the U.K.'s annual postal volume. The scale of the operation itself is a clear indication that the system has enabled Tesco to sell more of the right products to the right customers at the right prices.

In financial services, some banks have succeeded in gaining new clients without damaging their profitability by shaping offers around careful data mining. Instead of simply offering a lower interest rate to every potential new client, the bank offers lower rates only to clients that it sees as the most desirable new customers. This encourages the lower-risk client to sign up, while avoiding the trap of growing by taking on new higher-risk clients, which would reduce the bank's overall risk-adjusted return. At the same time, by mining the data of their existing customers, banks can also rank-order their customers based on their profit contributions and mete out services and fees accordingly.

Regardless of how well companies are doing with their targeted pricing, the practice is surely here to stay. This is because companies have a big incentive to charge different people different prices to increase their profitability, and technological progress is increasingly enabling companies to act on the incentives. However, as targeted pricing gains traction in the marketplace, the biggest risk facing practicing companies is that customers will become aware that another set of customers is paying much less for the same product or service. This may be especially true now, with the Internet and the ease with which thousands or even millions of consumers can learn about a pricing practice. Amazon, for instance, once faced a huge public relations challenge when regular customers felt annoyed that a discount applied only to "switchers," consumers who were defecting from another e-commerce site.

Of course, this risk is, in general, relatively low from the seller's perspective. Consumers do not necessarily pay attention to the prices of all goods they purchase. They also do not remember all the prices they pay. They surely do not talk about prices they pay for every product they purchase. And even if they know that they pay a different price, they do not necessarily get upset. Fortunately for companies, there's quite a bit of room in the marketplace to implement targeted pricing without worrying too much about adverse consumer reactions. (When was the last time you asked a passenger sitting next to you about the price he paid for his ticket?) Plus, even if some customers do catch on to the practice, the offerings can always be adjusted to make them less easily comparable.

Another risk in a price-targeting campaign is that the retailer might succeed too well in selecting only desirable customers. If competitors recognize what is happening, they may decide to work harder to poach what they now realize is a good client base. Sometimes bribe wars even break out. One of the most notorious cases of unintended consequences of such a campaign happened in the early 1990s in the epic battle between MCI and AT&T for long-distance customers. AT&T offered MCI customers a check of $25 to $100 for switching to AT&T. Not surprisingly, at least to observers outside AT&T, MCI struck back with a similar offer to AT&T subscribers. The end result was that millions of customers switched (perhaps multiple times!), pocketing checks every time they crossed the fence and undoubtedly becoming less loyal to either service with every jump.[37]

But just because this is how the targeted pricing game is played now doesn't mean this is the way it will always be played. Advances in analytics and new technologies such as cellphone-based coupons will likely keep changing the rules. In the future, we expect to see ever more sophisticated and innovative targeted pricing schemes, limited only by the marketer's creativity.

Interestingly, unlike many pricing strategies, targeted pricing need not favor big, dominant companies at the expense of small ones.

Earlier literature on targeted pricing often saw it as a form of leverage that a dominant company could use to squeeze and marginalize a smaller company. However, the complexity of today's competitive targeted pricing makes this strategy a tool that enables every company, regardless of market position, to compete with every other company for the customer's favor. Ironically, the more competitive the struggle for price advantage becomes, the more each company will succeed or fail based on the quality of its product or service. In that sense, technology is actually a great equalizer, forcing all companies to bare it all, so to speak, and face the judgment of consumers. In the long run, all this research should encourage more firms to become more customer-friendly and market-oriented, to the consumers' benefit.

Name Your Own Business Model

Price discrimination is a practice nearly as old as business itself. Over the history of modern retailing, companies have come up with many ingenious ways to screen customers so that they can profitably charge different prices to different segments of price sensitivity. From this perspective, Walker was exaggerating in describing Priceline as "the first new pricing system in probably 500 years." However, although it's easy to make fun of Walker's bombastic statements—especially in hindsight, knowing how bad so much of the highly hyped New Economy turned out—the fact is that, after the hype settled, he actually did create billions in genuine value with one simple pricing idea. As with Sy Syms and Edward Filene, Walker proved just how integral a creative pricing strategy can be, not just in selling a particular product, but in shaping a retailer's entire value proposition.

Walker may yet prove to be a prophet in pricing, however. His vision of a new world of dynamic pricing in which the value of retail goods fluctuates constantly and different people pay different prices for essentially the same goods and services is coming to pass. With modern communication and information technologies—and, more specifically, the widespread adoption of radio frequency identification (RFID) tags to track product flows—it is not hard to imagine that advances in customer-screening mechanisms, as represented by Priceline and the price-targeting methods we have discussed in this chapter, could soon come together to make dynamic retail pricing a reality. The day may soon come when a customer walks down a supermarket aisle and prices on the electronic monitors positioned next to the goods in the aisle start to change, in recognition of the purchase history of the customer, inventory levels of the goods at the time, number of customers in the store, or even the weather outside.

However, before we reach this world of floating prices, companies have years of experimentation ahead as they learn to generate increasingly compelling and unique offers to their customers and, at the same time, collect different types of customers with better precision. Walker's "name your own price" strategy is almost certainly only the first of many successes in matching the right offer with the right customer at the right profit-maximizing moment. Companies will continue to improve the way they segment customers efficiently and even identify the habits of individual customers on the fly. As a result, there will be many Priceline types of companies to be born. "Name your own price" is old hat now for consumers, but for the pricing entrepreneur, the opportunity to "name your own customer" is only beginning.

Endnotes

[1]Leonhardt, David, "Make a Cyber Bid But Don't Pack Your Bags," *BusinessWeek* (June 1, 1998).

[2]Ernst & Young, *Net Entrepreneurs Only*, (Hoboken, NJ: John Wiley Press, 2001), 5.

[3]Machan, Dyan,"An Edison for a New Age?" *Forbes* (May 17, 1999).

[4]Ernst & Young, 5.

[5]Ernst & Young, 5.

[6]Segan, Sascha, *Priceline For Dummies* (Hoboken, NJ: Wiley, 2005): 11.

[7]Griese, Noel L., *Crisis Counselor* (Tucker, Ga.: Anvil Publishers, 2004): 234.

[8]Price, Christopher, *The Internet Entrepreneurs* (Harlow, UK: FT Press, 2000): 42.

[9]Ernst & Young, 19.

[10]Williams, Kathy, "Tom D'Angelo Priceline.com's Mr. Inside" *Strategic Finance* (July 2002): 22.

[11]Conde Nast's Portfolio.com statistics.

[12]*Op cit .[Williams]*

[13]"Priceline 2.0," *BrandWeek* (March 6, 2006): 27.

[14]Wilner, Joshua, "Exclusive Interview: Priceline.com," *E-Commerce Times* (January 19, 2000).

[15]Jiang, Yabing, "Price Discrimination with Opaque Products," *Journal of Revenue and Pricing Management* (January 2007): 130.

[16]Bootle, Roger, *Money for Nothing* London: Nicholas Brealey Publishing, 2003): 238.

[17]Varian, Hal, "Priceline's Magic Show," *The Industry Standard* (April 24, 2000).

[18]Rothenberg, Randall, "Jay Walker: The Thought Leader Interview," *Strategy + Business* (Spring 2000).

[19]Varian, Hal, "A Model of Sales," *American Economic Review* 70 (1980): 651–659Conlisk, John; Gerstner, Eitan; and Sobel, JohnJohn Conlisk, Eitan Gerstner, and Joel Sobel, "Cyclic Pricing by a Durable Goods Monopolist," *Quarterly Journal of Economics* (August 1984): 489–505.

[20]Chen, Yuxin, Moorthy, Sridhar, and Zhang, Z. Hohn, "Research Note—Price Discrimination After the Purchase: Rebates as State-Dependent Discounts," Management Science 51 (no. 7): 1131–1140.

[21]Hahn, John-Hee "Damaged Durable Goods," *RAND Journal of Economics* (Spring 2006): 121–133.

[22]Promotions Marketing Association, Coupon Council, www.couponmonth.com.

[23]Kesmodel, David, "The Coupon King," *Wall Street Journal* (February 16, 2008): A-1.

[24]Hartnett, Michael, "Coupons Still King," *Frozen Food Age* (October 2006): 41.

[25]Cuneo, Alice Z., "Packaged Goods Giants Roll Out Mobile Coupons," *Advertising Age* (March 10, 2008): 3.

[26]Kesmodel, *WSJ*.

[27]*Ibid.*

[28]Jiang, "Discrimination" article—footnote 15.

[29]Zimmerman, Ann, "Wal-Mart Boosts Private Label to Court Thriftier Consumers,"*Wall Street Journal* (March 17, 2009).

[30]Rohwedder, Cecilie and Kesmodel, David, "Aldi Looks to U.S. for Growth," *Wall Street Journal* (January 13, 2009).

[32]*Ibid.*

[33]Moore, Pamela, "Will Priceline Need a Lifeline?" *BusinessWeek* (October 6, 2000).

[34]*Ibid.*

[35]Arthur C. Pigou, *The Economics of Welfare* (Macmillan, London, 1920).

[36]Rigby, Elizabeth, "Eyes in the Till," *Financial Times Magazine* (11–12 November 2006).

[37]Shaffer, Greg and Zhang, Z. John "Competitive One-to-One Promotions," *Management Science* 48 (no. 9): 1143–1160.

7

Subscribe and Save: Pricing for Marketing Profitability

"Pennywise, pound-foolish."
Old English adage

Every week, most of us walk out of the supermarket pushing a cart that contains almost the same things we bought the week before—breakfast cereals, coffee, bread, and dish soap. Supermarkets post the prices for each item they carry, and we pay the posted price for every item we purchase, usually without a second thought. When we get home, we may find that a magazine has come in the mail: Although we might buy the magazine on the newsstand, we choose instead to pay an annual or semiannual fee for the convenience of having our publications arrive like clockwork every day or week or month.

This seems normal to us, almost part of the natural order. Groceries you buy every week. Publications you subscribe to for months or a year at a time. Buy why? Why should it make more sense that we pay annually to read a publication every day, but we pay every week for the coffee we drink every day?

It turns out that there may be no good reason. In 2007, the often innovative Amazon.com began an experiment to let customers make their recurrent grocery purchases online. Amazon's Subscribe & Save program enables customers to choose the quantities of such routine purchases as coffee, breakfast cereals, shampoo, laundry detergent, and more, as well as the frequency with which they want the stock replenished. Then Amazon delivers to the customer the selected goods in the specified quantities and at the specified intervals. As Amazon describes it, the Subscribe & Save program is "a great way to save an extra 15% on items you use routinely—coffee, shampoo, laundry detergent, and more—while helping to make sure you don't run out." The products are priced at a bulk rate, sold for less than they would have been sold in a store, and shipped without a separate shipping charge. Amazon encourages customers to sign up for "subscriptions" but charges their credit card account stored with the company only when their recurring order ships. Consumers can change or cancel their orders at any time. In effect, Amazon is selling groceries as if they were newspapers or magazines: with subscription pricing.

On the surface, putting customers on subscription plans for recurring grocery purchases should be an intuitive idea, given that information, software, and other industries use subscription pricing. But grocery retailers have hardly experimented with subscription pricing at all, beyond the annual fees for becoming customers at buyers' clubs such as Costco. Breaking away from an entrenched pricing practice takes a good deal of innovative spirit, courage, and customer focus—all qualities that are in short supply in retailing, as in most industries.

In the grocery retailing industry, as in many other sectors, businesses typically have a fairly simple vision of how to turn a profit: put the product on a shelf, set a price, and then sell as many units as possible. Profit is simply the number of widgets or pounds of fresh vegetables or meat sold at a given price minus the cost of getting them to the shelf. For a grocer, for instance, total profit is the sum of the profits on each product he carries in his store. In other words, profit is the sum of the profits on each transaction made in a store for a product.[1] Suppose, for instance, that we own a grocery store that carries only two products: produce and meat. For produce, we have only two transactions. From the first transaction, we make $25 in gross profits, and from the second, we make $5. Altogether, produce has generated $30. For meat, let's suppose that we also have two transactions. From the first transaction, we make $35, and from the second, we also make $35. Altogether, we make $70 from meat. Our total gross profit from the store is then equal to $100 ($30 from produce plus $70 from meat), as shown in the following min-table. After subtracting some fixed costs for store rentals, salaries, and refrigeration, we can arrive at the store's net profit, the money that we, as the store owners, can pocket. (For the sake of simplicity, from this point on, we assume away any fixed cost so that the gross profit is the money we can take home.)

Profit Contributions

	Produce	**Meat**	
	$25	$35	
	$5	$35	
Gross Profit	$30	$70	Total: $100

At first glance, this chart seems very useful—it shows where the profits are coming from And tells us exactly what we should do : Meat is more profitable than produce, so we should care more about the meat department. It's a big profit center, after all.

But look at the numbers from a different angle. What this table conceals may be more important than what it reveals. The vertical summation focuses our attention on the individual categories. The act of summing up profits across all transactions for a given category reinforces a product-centric view of the business, a perception that the products are basically separate profit centers.

However, this view misses the linkages between products. Being overly focused on the most important element from our perspective—to sell products profitably—can actually obscure some important truths about the consumer. For instance, although these purchases show up in the data as isolated transactions, customers are actually buying many things at the same time. In the produce and meat example, for instance, as you read the information in the table, you likely did not question how transactions in each product category relate to each other. Yet common sense suggests such relationships clearly exist (steak *or* potatoes?).

More important, this product-centric view of profitability obscures the motives of customers, who may have had very different reasons to make their purchases—reasons we might capitalize on if we only thought about them for a minute. Nor does the damage that the product-centric view can inflict necessarily end there. As the saying goes, what you measure is what you see, and what you see is what you manage. A product-centric view of profitability inevitably shapes what you manage—and the more disciplined a manager you are, the more you will be blind to all kinds of other opportunities. Consider the example of produce versus meat: If we wanted to increase our grocery's profitability, we would try to lower the variable cost in each product category so that the gross profit from each transaction is bigger. For instance, maybe we would carry less quickly spoiling produce. We might also focus on increasing the number of transactions in each product category, perhaps through advertising or sale promotions. If our advertising budget is limited and we can advertise only one product, we would certainly choose to advertise meat because it is the more profitable product of the two. If we want to run a sales promotion, we would run the promotion on meat, as sales for that product category are more profitable and offer more room for a margin reduction.

In this product-centric world in which we simply count the beans all the time, it's hard to see why subscription pricing would be relevant. This is perhaps why grocery retailers have seldom considered subscription pricing.

However, if we change the angle from which we measure the profitability of the grocery and take a more customer-centric view, we might begin to see important patterns we overlooked before. For example, we might find that the first transaction in both product categories is made by a produce-focused customer who is attracted to your store because of the fresh produce we carry. If we don't keep fresh produce in our store, that customer will simply shop somewhere else. However, once in our store, that customer also purchases meat, to yield that nice profit of $35. Therefore, this customer makes a total profit contribution in the amount of $60, which we refer to as customer profitability in the next table. Similarly, the second transactions in both product categories are made by a meat-focused customer who cares about meat in your store but not so much about produce. The total profit contribution from this customer is $40. By changing our point of view, it's easy to see now that the produce-focused customer actually contributes a total profit of $60, $20 more than the meat-focused customer.

Profit Contributions

	Produce	**Meat**	**Customer Profitability**
Produce Focused	$25	$35	$60
Meat Focused	$5	$35	$40
Category Gross Profit	$30	$70	Total: $100

Note that the total profit for the store is still $100, and nothing has changed in these numbers. The only thing that has changed is the way we look at them: Instead of summing up vertically for a given product across different customers or transactions, we are summing up horizontally for a given customer across different products.

This change might seem technical, but it can have a dramatic effect. Shifting the axis gives us a totally different view of the business in terms of both what we know about the customer and what we should do to better manage our business. It allows us to move away from a product-centric view to a customer-centric view by putting customers right at the center of our profit summation.

Working from this view of profitability, we see, first, that the idea of touting meat in our promotions does not make much sense. After all, the produce-focused customer is more profitable. We really want to attract more produce-focused customers. If we can advertise only one product category, we'll want to push our store as a destination of fresh produce, even though more of our accounting profits come from meat. We may even want to use loss-leader pricing on produce, betting that low produce prices will help attract more of those profitable produce-focused customers.

This customer-centric view also helps us sell more meat as well, and identify other potential cross-selling opportunities. Through in-store marketing and floor arrangements, we can find ways to sell more produce to meat-focused customers, for example—or vice versa. Making this mental adjustment gives us a tremendous range of new opportunities—lower cost, higher potential opportunities than those afforded simply by monitoring accounting profit—all made clear simply by looking at the data from a different angle.

The customer-focused profitability metric also makes it possible to increase profitability without having to arm-twist our customers for a bigger margin or more sales. This customer-focused view enables us to tap into an endless source of opportunity: Any actual retail operation has many more than two kinds of customers. In fact, even the same customer might behave differently in different contexts. Despite many regular habits, customers buy different things depending on the occasion and exhibit different behavioral patterns in different categories—for example, a value shopper in dairy products might be a luxury shopper in chocolate. By recognizing customers' buying behaviors and tracking their purchase patterns over time, we can identify a whole range of products that might appeal to the same customer now and in the future. All these new customer insights give us greater flexibility in designing promotions and pricing incentives that will motivate customers to give us larger and increasingly profitable sales.

Through the lens of customer-centric profitability, it becomes less difficult to see how Amazon sensed an opportunity for innovative pricing by selling mundane groceries. Amazon realized that a large share of consumers' grocery baskets are filled with products they buy every week or month—as much as 85% by some estimates.[22] Through subscriptions, Amazon could capture a huge share of the customers' pantry. Instead of trying to wring the most money possible out of each transaction from each product, the way an unsophisticated grocer might, Amazon uses subscription pricing to extend the breadth, depth, and duration of its relationship with customers. Such a pricing format not only motivates customers to enter into a relationship, but also cements that relationship. Indeed, assuming that Amazon's fulfillment is excellent (a safe assumption at this point, given its large network of distribution centers), the recurrent performance even helps build trust in the Amazon brand as a seller of other, higher-margin items.

Capturing these recurrent sales gives Amazon a number of strategic advantages. Buyers essentially put their future core purchases on autopilot. As a result, subscription pricing reduces short-term competitive pricing pressure by reducing customers' needs to make frequent buying decisions. It puts competitors on the defensive because an ongoing relationship takes up space, time, and money, in the same way as any other subscription. If you already subscribe to one newspaper, you're less likely to buy another at the newsstand. Similarly, if you know you have another shipment of paper towels coming in tomorrow, you're less likely to pick some up on the way home from work tonight, even if they're on sale. This is good news for Amazon because the subscription model creates a recurring revenue stream that varies less by season and buyer whims. Best of all, after customers become used to the convenience of regular Amazon deliveries, Amazon might be able to open the door to other purchases, both inside and outside the Subscribe & Save channel. Furthermore, the subscription model creates a recurring revenue stream that varies less by season and buyer whims.

Only time will tell whether Amazon's Subscribe & Save program succeeds. However, maintaining this kind of customer focus in its pricing decisions can only improve Amazon's chances for success. Already, customer profitability seems to be leading Amazon to new opportunities in other areas. Consider how another new program, Amazon Prime, is overcoming the problem of shipping costs, which have always been a huge problem in direct-to-consumer sales. Traditionally, most direct-to-consumer companies have solved this problem in one of two ways, either by charging a fee based on actual cost of shipment or by making it a profit center. Others have tried to make it a profit, assuming that the "sticker" price on the website or the catalog is usually the one about which the consumer is most aware. Generally, a correct assumption.

However, analysts have found that neither approach is wholly satisfactory. Most of the time, the "sticker" price is what matters most, but analysts have found this is not true for all consumers. This is certainly true for Amazon. For occasional buyers, shipping costs may not matter much. For heavy users, however, the cost of shipping becomes an important consideration. Like many other direct-to-consumer companies, Amazon has always offered free shipping over a certain price range. This has encouraged some kinds of buying, but it has not encouraged buyers to make Amazon the store of first resort for a broad range of products. Amazon Prime eliminates the issue by offering free two-day shipping in exchange for a $79 annual membership fee. The ingenious plan not only levels the playing field between Amazon and ordinary retailers, but it also simultaneously makes the customer more invested in her relationship with Amazon than with other online retail sites: After shelling out $79, most customers will want to get their money's worth out of the membership and by ordering more from Amazon.

The $79 membership fee is also hefty enough that it acts as a sorting mechanism to keep out less frequent (and less profitable) online shoppers. If a customer is not a frequent online buyer, she would not want to pay that $79 membership fee up front. Thus, Amazon has found a way to deliver a low shipping cost to its most profitable customers—and simultaneously use that benefit to lock them in.

The lock the membership fee creates is an important part of the strategy because the goal isn't just to get the customer to buy more—it's to get the customer to spend more time at the site and buy something more valuable, to think of Amazon not just as a bookstore, for example, but as an electronics dealer. "If you pay $79 for a membership, then you'll say, well, if I want to buy a digital camera, maybe I'll look at Amazon," explains CEO Jeff Bezos. "It gets people to start checking across categories."[3]

The company hasn't released too many details about the success of the program, but the fact that the company has now rolled out Amazon Prime internationally indicates that it is probably working. One analyst estimates that more than 3.44 million Amazon customers signed up for Prime accounts by the end of 2007, heavy users who generated as much as 25% of Amazon's total sales.[4]

The Bigger Picture

The customer-centric view of profitability we have been discussing is a specific application of the concept of "marketing profitability," a profitability metric that accounts for customer buying behaviors and patterns in a way that is consistent with the conventional metric of accounting profitability. The metric can be applied in many different ways, depending on the industry and the intensity of competition. However, marketing profitability isn't good simply for picking out opportunities. It's also a useful tool for avoiding missteps. Just as a close look at a balance sheet can show a trained eye that what appears to be a booming business is in fact on the verge of collapse, a marketing profitability perspective can help a company expose strategic missteps that might be hard to spot quarter by quarter.

For example, an analysis of one supermarket chain in terms of its marketing profitability (defined in this case as the store-wide profitability attributable to the existence of a product category), found a wide range in the marketing profitability of the store's ten super categories. Produce was no. 1 in terms of marketing profitability—unsurprising, perhaps, because quality produce plays a large part of how consumers select a grocery store, and these consumers go on to buy many products in other categories that contribute to the store's total profitability. However, in four super categories—Dairy, Meat, Deli, and Bakery—marketing profits were actually negative, which implies that the presence of these four product categories in the store adds negatively to the store's overall profitability. This is a huge surprise, given that only the Bakery generates a conventional accounting loss.

What does negative marketing profitability mean? Accounting losses are simple to understand. When you don't sell enough of Product X to cover the cost of the product and the overhead, the store loses money on the product. But what does a marketing profitability loss mean? Negative marketing profitability occurs when customers who are attracted to the store for a particular product spend little on anything outside of that product or spend a lot on items that are not profitable to the retailer but for which the carrying costs are very high. Essentially, marketing profitability shows how strong—or weak—the coattails of a given category are. At the same time, marketing profitability can reveal if a particular product is attracting the wrong kind of customer to a store.[5]

After examining the retailer's business through the two lenses of accounting profitability and marketing profitability, we can divide the store's entire stock into four basic divisions. Some products have a high accounting profit (a large difference between revenues and costs for the product) but a low marketing profit. A lucky few have a high accounting profit as well as a high marketing profit. Others have a low accounting profit but a high marketing profit. Finally, some have both low (or even negative) accounting and marketing profits. This new perspective gives the retailer an important tool to clarify not just the right price and product mix, but any number of supportive business practices.

Of course, a product that has a high accounting profit and marketing profit is a star for the retailer and is worthy of the retailer's promotion expenditures. On the other hand, a product that has a high accounting profit but a low marketing profit is essentially an add-on product for consumers. Its profit contribution to the store is limited to its own sales. This means that in-store marketing to increase the category's sales is the key to maximizing the product's profit potential, not promotions designed to draw more customers to the store. The reverse, however, is not always the case. Marketing profitability analysis sometimes suggests retaining a product that has a low or negative accounting profit if its marketing profit is high. Such a product may even be a good candidate for effective loss-leader pricing. However, if the product is losing money and also has a low (or negative) marketing profit, the retailer should seriously think about why it should continue to give it any shelf space.

Marketing profitability can also be a good metric to build employee incentives around because it encourages thinking not just within the confines of one department or category, but about that category's role in the entire store. For example, in one of the grocery store studies cited earlier, beauty aids earned only $76 in accounting profits during the data period for each linear footage of shelf space allocated but generated huge marketing profits: $9,378.

The Mouse That Roared

The concept of marketing profitability is not only useful for retailers such as Amazon. Other kinds of businesses can benefit as well.

Even entertainment leviathans have made big gains through marketing profitability. For instance, marketing profitability offered a fresh perspective that helped drive the extraordinary growth of revenue in Disney's theme parks in the 1980s.

By the early 1980s, Disney's theme parks (in Anaheim, California, and Orlando, Florida) were already beloved institutions. The Walt Disney Company had skillfully promoted the parks through shorts that accompanied its movies and long-running television shows for such a long time that they had come to be seen not just as amusement parks, but almost as a kind of mecca for children and their families. The experience even began to take on an almost religious significance for many, a sort of rite of childhood. One sign of their early importance: Kodak has estimated that 5% of all the pictures taken in North America are taken at one of the Disney parks.[6]

Then as now, millions of families spent thousands of dollars each year for the chance to take amusement park rides in a landscape based on the Disney movies and the pantheon of Disney characters. In 1984, the parks attracted 30 million visitors, each of them shelling out $18.95 for entrance, not to mention food and souvenirs.

But when Michael Eisner, the brash 42-year-old CEO, took charge at Disney in 1984, he didn't see the mature, profitable business that others saw. Instead, he saw that Disney had built a Magic Kingdom of profit for other people—specifically, for the many outside-owned hotels and other businesses that had sprung up around the parks to serve them.

For anyone reviewing the parks' accounting profitability, the numbers looked stunning. However, Eisner looked beyond the accounting numbers, into the buying behaviors and purchasing patterns of his customers, and realized that Disney had actually captured a relatively small share of the billions of dollars Disney visitors brought to Orlando every year.

Although visitors came to Orlando with their wallets loaded and the theme park as their destination, Disney managed to capture only a fraction of the total expense involved in visiting Disney World—perhaps just 25% of visitors' vacation dollars.[7] To get more out of all these devoted Mousketeers, Eisner proposed several measures. The first move was to increase the park's admissions. As so many customers had already invested heavily to fly all the way to Orlando to visit the park, he saw no reason Disney could not raise its ticket prices. Entrance fees stood at $18.95 for the day in 1985, a number he pushed in gradual steps up to $28 in 1988, a $310 million annual gain in operating profit over four years with virtually no adverse publicity. Next, Eisner began expanding Disney's hotels and restaurants. As one case study put it, "Unconstrained by any conventional definitions or concepts of what an entertainment company is supposed to do, he invested in different components of the retailing and vacation value chains, fundamentally reshaping Disney's business design."[8]

By 1990, the Disney parks generated $3 billion in revenue, more than either entertainment ($2.2 billion) or consumer products ($574 million).[9] And Disney had tripled its share of visitors' wallets: The company estimated that it now captured 75% of visitor's dollars.[10]

Today the company is perfecting the art of capturing the lion's share of a visitor's expenditures. It pitches packaged visits to the theme parks across a wide range of travel segments, from Disney Deluxe Villas ("comfortable accommodations with all the conveniences of home") to Disney Value Resorts ("colorful, whimsical places that are big on fun but small on cost"), and even campgrounds. A Disney vacation is not cheap—currently, the cost of a four-day, three-night holiday ranges from $1,236 to $3,640, not including a meal plan[11]—but customers keep coming, and the company continues to get high marks for service.

Beyond the range in overall cost, the packages show a tremendous sensitivity to a variety of customer preferences. They include conveniences that can be very attractive to parents with more kids and bags than arms, such as luggage delivery direct to their hotel room and shuttle buses from their hotel to the park gates. Another particularly prized benefit at Walt Disney World is the right to enter one of the parks each day either early, before it opens to the general public, or late, after it closes—a valuable benefit, given the crush of the crowds and Orlando's sometimes brutal midday heat. Interestingly, although this is packaged as a benefit for guests, this benefit also helps balance the load in the busy parks over the course of a day. As with many marketing profitability initiatives, such as Amazon Prime, Disney profits partly by trading on unused scale capacities.

Together, these initiatives pulled customers further behind the walls of the Magic Kingdom and kept them there. The last time we visited Orlando with our family, we stayed inside Disney World and never managed to get out of it. In the end, Disney captured nearly 100% of our expenditures!

Disney's marketing profitability thinking didn't end simply with capturing more of the wallet share of families visiting the theme parks. Disney planners have launched new products in pursuit of other parts of the travel markets as well, including executive education (the Disney Institute), corporate meetings, and other travel experiences, such as a Disney-branded cruise line. Operating income of the parks and resorts segment has grown to $11.5 billion.[12] None of that would have happened if Eisner had not converted the company to a strategy driven by the full view of the consumer that a marketing profitability perspective demands, which looked first at Disney's share of a Disney vacation, and now at Disney's share of *travel*.

Using marketing profitability as a share of customer expenditure to reimagine a market isn't limited to companies in the fantasy business. Looked at by most angles, Wal-Mart is a global giant that can't possibly grow much more. In 2008, the company made $378 billion in revenues, making it the largest of the Fortune 500. For a long time, investors have questioned how much bigger Wal-Mart could become. To address that concern, Wal-Mart might look not at accounting revenues or profits, but its share of customer retail purchases. Through that lens, Wal-Mart's share of retail sales is actually fairly small, only 8% of all U.S. retail sales, giving the company a lot of room to grow.

Viewed in that light, Wal-Mart becomes once more a scrappy contender instead of a colossus that's far ahead of most of its competitors. Apparently Wal-Mart understands this, too—hence its relentless drive to carry more product categories, expand into new retail businesses, move into urban centers, and test different store formats.

McDonald's is another company that has made tremendous gains by making this shift in perspective. Instead of looking at the fast food landscape and seeing itself surrounded by smaller, weaker competitors, McDonald's looked toward a different, customer-focused metric: share of stomach.

McDonald's sells more than 4 million hamburgers a day in United States and has sold more than 100 billion hamburgers in the 50-plus years it has been in business. Where is the growth opportunity for the company? If you look through a marketing profitability lens, the answer is: everywhere. In 2008, McDonald's total revenues were about $23.5 billion, which qualified the company as the 106th-largest company among the Fortune 500 companies and as the Fortune 500's biggest food service company. However, relative to the total food expenditure of about $1.165 trillion in the United States, McDonald's captures only a tiny share. Even relative to the away-from-home food expenditure of $422 billion, McDonald's has a long way to go to claim a significant share. This new point of view made it clear to McDonald's executives that their biggest challenge was not really fending off Wendy's or Burger King, but getting more people to spend more time and money at Mickey D's.

The simplest way McDonald's has done this is to get customers to spend more. Just as Disney did with its entrance fees, McDonald's has made a concerted effort to gradually raise its prices. Between 2001 and 2005, for example, McDonald's managed to raise the price of the average check by a healthy but gradual percentage—1.9% in 2000, nothing in 2001, 2.1% in 2002, and 5% in both 2004 and 2005. For the individual customer, it was hardly noticeable, but gradual increases multiplied by a large number of customers added a lot of gold to the Golden Arches: Over that same period, revenue increased from $14.9 billion to $20.5 billion.

McDonald's has also tried to work on a temporal dimension, by trying to boost frequency. One of its most successful initiatives in this regard is the Happy Meal, perhaps the most brilliant bundling strategy of the last 30 years. Initially copied from a concept invented by a small regional fast food chain, the Happy Meal launched nationally in 1978. McDonald's executives found that by marketing a kid-size meal along with a small toy in an attractive box, they could greatly increase sales. The logic was pretty simple, and it was soon joined by a later successful initiative to bring in children: an indoor playground, that functioned on the same logic: "Playlands bring in children, who bring in parents, who bring in money," one observer explained.[13]

The new Happy Meal consisted of a colorful cardboard box that contained a burger or chicken nuggets, fries, a drink, and a toy. The toy was crucial. The toy boosted the perceived value of the meal and also led to repeat sales, such as the sales of train sets that required a visit every week. In one of the most extreme cases, a 1997 promotion for Beanie Babies, a collection of small stuffed collectible animals, enthusiasm rose so quickly for the Beanie Babies that McDonald's eventually sold 100 million Happy Meals in a ten-day period, ten times more than normal.[14] That's roughly four Happy Meals for every child in America. In fact, a lot of those meals were probably purchased by adult collectors who threw the food in the garbage, a group that, over time, has become a second important market for Happy Meals.

In its 30 years of existence, the Happy Meal formula has not changed appreciably. In the United States, the box now includes a healthy dessert, and some countries offer other food options (in China, for instance, kids may order a cheese-and-egg sandwich on a steamed bun instead of a hamburger).[15] But no matter where the Happy Meal is sold, everyone still gets that all-important toy, a product that's not even on the menu. Worldwide, the company gives away 1.5 billion toys every year. In the United States alone, one of every three toys comes from McDonald's.[16] Incredibly, the toy prize has become so successful that McDonald's is now the largest toy distributor in the world. "McDonald's is in some ways a toy company, not a food company," says one retired fast food executive. He is not exaggerating. The toys are big business for McDonald's: A successful toy can boost sales 4%, and a hit, such as the Beanie Babies, can send total sales up as much as 15%, according to industry analysts—not a bad return on a 30¢–50¢ trinket.[17]

Today the company is using marketing profitability analysis to reinvent itself once more, this time to attract a different set of customers: high-end coffee drinkers. The pioneer of fast food is rapidly reengineering itself as a place for a slow sip—the kind of spot sociologists call "a third place," that's neither work nor home, but shares some qualities of both. Following Starbucks' lead, McDonald's is trying to capitalize on the consumer's desire for a pleasant, affordable place to have a high-quality coffee. Since 2004, the decor of more than 40% of McDonald's restaurants have been redecorated as a place to linger, with more comfortable chairs, natural lighting and materials, Wi-Fi, and a gourmet coffee drink.[18] This new module, McCafé, a sub-brand set up within the larger restaurant, is proving very popular in Europe, where there are now more than 1,000 units. McCafé has 500 units in Germany alone, making it already the most popular coffeehouse in the country.

Even more exciting to executives is the fact that the McCafé line actually seems to grow sales not just of coffee and breakfast pastries, but of ordinary Big Macs and hamburgers. McCafés seem to attract a different set of customers who seldom ate there before. Most McDonald's outlets in Germany that have installed redecorated McCafés, the new shop-within-a-shop is generating 12%–15% more sales in Germany—and, in some cases, as much as 20% more. "Suddenly, we're playing in a totally different league," says Holger Beeck, Director of Operations for McDonald's Germany.[19] Just as the toys brought children who brought in families, coffee is now bringing in adults with money.

Another sign that the company is again looking more at marketing profitability than accounting profitability is the upscale price being charged for the coffee. Traditionally, McDonald's has appealed to price-sensitive customers. One of the reasons the lights were bright and the seats not especially comfortable was undoubtedly to keep the crowds moving and to discourage the homeless from camping out. But instead of competing on price, McDonald's is choosing to compete as a Starbucks alternative. Coffees at McCafé are actually just slightly cheaper than at Starbucks, their biggest competitor. In New York, for instance, a 20-ounce flavored coffee is priced at $4.22, just 13¢ less than a similar drink in the same-size Starbucks cup.[20]

Breakfast, lunch, dinner, and now coffee: Isn't this the end for McDonald's? No. It's hard to say where it might grow next, but undoubtedly new possibilities are waiting to be uncovered as McDonald's grabs more share of stomach. One may ask why, after all, McDonald's products are sold only in its outlets. For instance, why couldn't the company also sell frozen desserts and hamburgers through grocers' freezers? Or ethnic foods? Campbell soups? Indeed, Starbucks is already making similar extensions. One thing you can bet on is that McDonald's will continue to monitor the slightest changes in the consumption habits of its targeted customers and adjust its menus to capitalize on them.

The True Bottom Line

Companies set their prices to maximize their profitability. Therefore, it should come as no surprise that the way in which we measure profitability conditions what business opportunities we see and how we can capitalize on those opportunities. The examples from Amazon and other companies discussed in this chapter show that a marketing profitability perspective offers a great way to see gaps in an existing offering or the potential for an entirely new line. It is also a great way to streamline a pricing structure to accommodate and influence consumer buying behavior.

Amazon's subscription pricing for groceries is particularly noticeable to us because it is the last place one would think of using subscription pricing. However, as we gain more flexibility in thinking about profitability and move away from day-to-day sales imperatives to focus more on customers, it should become much easier to identify and seize the opportunities the way Amazon and these other companies did.

Such opportunities are endless. Recently, we've noticed that subscription pricing has also helped solve a problem most movie theaters have: how to boost attendance between blockbusters. To solve this problem, the two largest theater chains in France have taken a marketing profitability approach by making it more attractive for frequent moviegoers to go to the movies even in a month with few new releases. Gaumont and Pathé offer a movie pass for €18.90 a month—payable, significantly, only as part of a 12-month contract. Similar to the Amazon Prime program, the pass serves two functions: It creates a sunk cost that holders feel obliged to use often to get their money's worth, while at the same time reducing the attractiveness of other alternatives by making the pass feel "free." Assuming that the issue of paying the studios could be resolved, as it has apparently been resolved in France, it's hard to see why such a plan wouldn't work just as well in the United States.[21] Thinking along the same line, Starbucks may be well advised to put many of its regular customers on a subscription plan to prevent them from being poached by the competition.

Pricing for marketing profitability does not, of course, mean that you always want to put customers on a continuity or long-term contract. General Electric for instance, prices some of its industrial engines by hour in service. This is a compelling proposition for a user because it reduces the financial risk of an engine failing. It's also useful for GE, as it encourages the customer to think of GE as a long-time partner, not a company that will disappear when the warranty expires. The latest trend in software, cloud computing, is also being sold now on a usage basis; customers can more easily justify a purchase because takes a fixed cost, such as sales contact software, and transforms into a variable cost. Behind the cloud other services, too, can profit from similar pricing strategies.

Pricing with an eye toward marketing profitability demands a lot from the marketer. It's a difficult exercise that's easy to get wrong because consumers are complex to analyze and change all the time. However, as the cases in this chapter suggest, pricing for marketing profitability can be well worth the trouble. A marketing profitability focus keeps a company looking ahead as it defines and redefines its value proposition, probing, questioning, and asking repeatedly, "Who are our customers? What are we selling?" At the same time, it reduces the risk that, over time, the company will turn inward and become obsessed solely with its own internal workings. Or as Jeff Bezos once put it:

> Companies get skills-focused, instead of customer-needs focused. When [companies] think about extending their business into some new area, the first question is "[W]hy should we do that—we don't have any skills in that area." That approach puts a finite lifetime on a company because the world changes, and what used to be cutting-edge skills have turned into something your customers may not need anymore. A much more stable strategy is to start with "What do my customers need?" Then do an inventory of the gaps in your skills.[22]

And, we might add, price your offerings to accommodate and influence consumer buying behaviors to truly maximize your profit.

Endnotes

[1]Drawn from Chen, Yuxin, Hess, James D., Wilcox, Ronald T., Zhang, Z. John, "Accounting Profits Versus Marketing Profits: A Relevant Metric for Category Management," *Marketing Science* 18 (no. 3) (1999): 208–229.

[2]Lisante, April, *Philadelphia Daily News* (May 1, 2008).

[3]Hoff, Rob, "Amazon's Prime Challenge," *BusinessWeek* (February 12, 2009).

[4]Unbundling As a Pricing Strategy blog, "Bundling—Amazon Prime," http://unpundling.wordpress.com, January 2009.

[5]Chen, Hess, Wilcox, and Zhang, 210.

[6]Capodagli, Bill and Jackson, Lynn, *The Disney Way: Harnessing the Management Secrets of Disney in Your Company* (New York: McGraw-Hill Professional, 2006): 185.

[7]Young, Roy A., et al., *Marketing Champions* (New York: Wiley, 2006).

[8]Chen, Hess, Wilcox, and Zhang, 368.

[9]Peck, Helen, et al., *Relationship Marketing* (Oxford: Butterworth-Heineman, 1999).

[10]Young, 57.

[11]Disneyworld.disney.go.com (2009 vacation packages).

[12]Walt Disney Corporation Annual Report 2008.

[13]Wood, Ron, *Into the Value Zone: Gaining and Sustaining Competitive Advantage* (Lanham, Md.: University Press, 2008): 93.

[14]Oxoby, Marc, *The 1990s* (Westport, CT: Greenwood Publishing, 2003): 128.

[15]Barnes, David, *Operations Management* (London: Cengage Learning EMA, 2008): 391.

[16]Schlosser, Eric and Wilson, Charles, *Chew On This*, (New York: Houghton Mifflin, 2007).

[17]Barnes, Julian E., "Fast Food Giveaway Toys Face Recalls," *New York Times* (August 15, 2001).

[18]McDonald's Annual Report 2008.

[19]Food Service Europe.com, "McCafé: Coffee & Cake, a Growth Module" (February 5, 2009).

[20]Boyle, Christina, "Look What's Brewin': Mickey D's Bucks Up Joe Biz...," *Daily News* (April 17, 2009): 10.

[21]www.cinemasgaumontpathe.com.

[22]Jena McGregor, "Bezos on Innovation," *BusinessWeek* (April 17, 2008).

8

The Snob Premium

"You get what you pay for."
Anonymous

In the 1960s, paying with cards such as Diner's Club or American Express offered not just convenience, but cachet: Carrying a credit card implied a certain degree of status. Card providers made money mostly from annual fees.

As the market grew, competition drove those fees down. Not only did virtually everyone end up with a credit card, but most consumers carried multiple cards. Between 1997 and 2005 alone, card volume grew by 40%, from 1.80 cards per capita to 2.53. To survive, most card companies changed their business model.[1] The smartest saw themselves as providers of a commodity and knew that when trying to sell a commodity, the best strategy is usually to expand the market as wide as possible and sell the product for as little as possible. They reduced or eliminated the annual fee and began to make their money on other fees—most of all, on interest paid for running balances. As annoying as the extra fees could be to consumers, they grew into a big business for the credit card companies: Every year, those fees generate more than $11 billion in the United States alone.[2]

But even as most companies fought over the broad market share, a few began to differentiate their cards again on price—and in a surprising way, given that the industry had already driven their fees down to zero. They set an extremely high price. Through high price alone, they transformed what consumers had begun to call "plastic"—a generic financial product—back into a status symbol.

From Cash to Cachet

Perhaps the best known of this kind of premium card is the Centurion, the black American Express card. Launched in 1999, the invitation-only Centurion was marketed first to capitalize on an urban legend about a mythical black card for the ultra rich that allowed the bearer to purchase anything at any price, even private jets. Not coincidentally, the fee for the real card is $2,500 a year, with a $5,000 initiation fee. And it's definitely exclusive: Only 17,000 people pack the card in their wallet. Although membership includes a variety of benefits, such as airline class upgrades and invitations to such celebrity-oriented events as a chance to play a round of golf with Tiger Woods, the biggest benefit is reportedly a certain nontangible sense of specialness that goes along with plinking the titanium card down on the counter. As one card holder told CNN.com, he "enjoys the star treatment the card affords him."[3]

Following Amex's success, other card companies have followed suit. In 2004, Coutts & Co. (a private British bank that counts Queen Elizabeth II among its clients) introduced a purple card for its high-net-worth customers.[4] In December 2008, perhaps to take away some business from Amex as the credit crunch hit, Visa launched a $495 premium card that it calls "the Black Card." Its website (www.blackcard.com) describes it as a product designed "[f]or those who demand only the best of what life has to offer .... The Black Card is not just another piece of plastic. Made with carbon graphite, it is the ultimate buying tool."

This kind of premium pricing for financial services seems to work even without titanium or carbon graphite. High-net-worth investors often pay more for financial services that don't actually outperform much cheaper alternatives. For instance, high-fee separately managed accounts have grown even though many of the underlying investments perform no better than a low-fee index fund or a basket of exchange-traded funds.

Although some investors might have separately managed accounts for performance-related reasons (most of which have to do with the tax advantages of owning stock directly instead of owning it as a share of a mutual fund), much of the value of the product seems to be in the sense of specialness the SMA creates. "One of the things that separately managed accounts do for you is that they really give you status and whatever comes from status—a sense of power, of control, a sense of being special," explains Meir Statman, a behavioral economist at the University of Santa Clara, Santa Clara, California.[5]

This seems like quite an assertion, but one point that suggests Statman is right about what marketers call the "expressive" benefits of SMAs is the fact that although computers have made it possible to manage much smaller accounts separately now for years, accounts with minimums of less than six figures have not really caught on in the market.[6]

Further up the wealth ladder, the popularity of hedge funds also can be explained in part by a desire for status. True, certain strategies, such as short portfolios, are open only to hedge funds and generally not mutual funds. However, as with the SMA example, the possibility of satisfying status desires seems to be part of the package. We know this because although some hedge funds outperform the stock market, very few actually succeed. A 2005 survey of 1994–2004 data found that even the best hedge funds outperform for only a few years before reverting to the mean. The only consistent performers were the consistently bad.[7]

In fact, the sole way hedge funds outperform year in and year out is in their fees. When it comes to fees, hedge funds are at the top of the class. Standard terms are 2% of assets annually, plus at least 20% of any profits, an arrangement that can cost up to 3.5% of assets a year.[8] Some charge more: Star investment manager James Simon reportedly charges 5% of assets and 44% of returns.[9] On top of that, other financial advisors often take another slice of 2%–3% a year in exchange for their due diligence in selecting managers.

Most of the time, the high fees are seen primarily as a necessary evil—the incentive needed to retain the best and the brightest money managers. But as with the black credit cards, the high sticker price also adds to the status and mystique, both essential qualities, given the funds' actual performance.

Indeed, high fees and a low profile have tended to be part of the hedge fund mystique all the way back to their invention by Alfred Winslow Jones in 1948. Jones, a freelance writer, had the idea after interviewing a number of technical stock analysts for a *Fortune* magazine article titled "Fashions in Forecasting." Jones's simple but innovative concept was to create what he called a "hedged fund," a portfolio that combined long positions in undervalued stocks with short positions in overvalued stocks, reducing the overall risk in investing either short or long.[10] Two months before the article went to press, he launched a $100,000 fund with three friends based on this idea.[11]

Jones's scholarly training at Columbia (he had earned a Ph.D. in sociology before the Depression pushed him into journalism) formed the foundation of his business in two ways. First, Jones copied the fee structure—20% of the gains—from that of an investment fund of a friend he had made at Columbia, the legendary investor and finance professor Benjamin Graham.[12] Second, the fact that Jones was an intellectual himself seems to have been an important ingredient in the success of his fund: A number of his early investors were writers and artists, who might have added some cachet to the product while keeping it somewhat removed from Wall Street—people who would actually understand more about what he was doing and presumably be less in awe of it. From the beginning, Jones made exclusivity part of the package: "[P]artnership in a hedge fund, particularly *the* hedge fund, was like membership in a highly desirable club. It certified one's affluence while attesting to one's astuteness."[13]

A carefully crafted low profile also helped accentuate the mystique. Part of the low profile was required: Then as now, securities laws wouldn't permit direct solicitation to the public. The rest had to do with Jones, who operated his fund with "spectacular success and in relative secrecy"[14] until his story hit *Fortune*. Most stories about Jones dismissed his penchant for secrecy as the eccentric personal preference of someone with a scholarly bent, but it seems an unlikely trait in a man who had interviewed hundreds, even thousands of people first as a sociologist and later as a journalist. The truth is the low profile worked well in marketing an exclusive product, a fact that couldn't have been lost on a former financial journalist.

One detail in particular suggests that Jones knew exactly what he was doing. Instead of using a staff photo for the groundbreaking *Fortune* story, Jones chose a picture of himself that his wife had taken in Mexico City, with palm trees in the background, looking a little like a character from a spy movie, which probably added to the air of mystery. The first major article in the fund's first 18 years, a 1966 piece in *Fortune*, "The Jones Nobody Keeps Up With," also described Jones as "seldom photographed," reinforcing the impression of exclusivity.

Those same marketing tools—high fees and an air of mystery— are still some of the most potent sales devices in what has grown into a $2 trillion industry. Why would anyone pay 4%–6% a year for returns that are often the same as or even worse than the returns offered by index funds that charge a tenth of that? For the same reason someone might pay $2,500 for a credit card: Statman has long argued that, as with other kinds of services, financial services offer "expressive benefits" to their buyers. He explains it this way:

> Expressive characteristics in products and services let us identify our values, our social class, and our life-style, and convey them to ourselves and to others. Expressive characteristics also add meaning to products and services beyond utilitarian characteristics.[15]

Looked at from this point of view, the people the Securities and Exchange Commission classifies as "sophisticated investors" who pay for SMAs and hedge funds aren't really paying extra money for nothing. They're deriving a certain kind of value out of the experience of being a client—a sense of membership in an exclusive strata of society.

Special Neighbors

As Jones's example suggests, part of the excitement of having his firm manage your money had to do with reasons other than the product itself—what Statman describes as an expressive benefit. The other interesting aspect of Jones' fund and many other high-price products is what economists call a positive externality—in this case, the chance to rub elbows with some bright and successful people. It's not exactly a new idea: An ancient Chinese story sums up a phenomenon that's still alive and well in many places and contexts:

> Once upon a time in China, a prominent scholar paid 1000 tael for a house. Not so long afterward, a merchant moved in next door. At one point, the two met and, as neighbors would, started discussing the price of real estate.
>
> "How much did you pay?" the scholar asked.
>
> "Nine thousand tael," said his new neighbor.
>
> "But I only paid 1,000 for mine, and that wasn't long ago," said the startled scholar. "Why did you pay so much?"
>
> "I paid 1,000 tael for the house, same as you," the merchant said.
>
> "What about that extra 8,000?"
>
> "That I paid for the neighbor!"

Of course, marketers in the West also know the importance of neighbors and further that under the right circumstances, price itself can help attract desirable neighbors. As with black credit cards and hedge funds, a high price can help create that mystique.

The case of Trump Tower is an illustration of how this process can work at the high end. When Donald Trump developed his 58-story skyscraper at 56th Street and Fifth Avenue in New York in 1983, he decided to market the entire product as a luxury destination: luxury shops below, luxury apartments above.

To help build some cachet for the complex, Trump took a big risk. He would try to sell the apartments far above market prices, at "the highest prices ever paid by man"[16]: $5 million for a four-bedroom apartment, which was still a lot of money in 1983. Trump's theory was that people at the stratospheric end of the market are basically insensitive about price, but they're very sensitive about the company they keep and the status they enjoy. In the stratosphere, he gambled that price becomes more important as a kind of velvet rope that separates one social group from another rather than as a measure of value. In fact, for a certain strata, overpaying might actually help screen residents and create that aura of specialness.

Trump's bet worked. Liberace bought the first apartment sold in the tower. Johnny Carson soon followed. Living next door to big entertainment and big money proved irresistible to others as well. The project was a success, and Trump as a brand name in real estate was born!

Of course, success with this kind of pricing in real estate depends on the seller finding a group of people who want to express their wealth publicly. In markets with more ambivalence toward public displays of wealth, this might not work as well. For instance, one developer in China tried the same strategy but failed because the society does not yet encourage conspicuous consumption. Being grouped into a single community did not make people feel special; it made them feel vulnerable. They might have been thinking less of the scholarly neighbor story than of a darker Chinese proverb about the dangers of being exceptional: *When hunting birds, you kill the one that flies out of the bush first.*

High prices can create value for the customer in other ways, too. In cosmetics, for example, a high price sometimes makes it easier to believe in what one plastic surgeon describes as "a miracle in a tightly

wrapped cellophane box with nice writing on it." Many women buy
lotions and creams that cost hundreds or even thousands of dollars—
some made with costly ingredients, such as gold or pearl. Asked why
she pays AU$690 (US$575 at the time) for a 50mL jar of Lauder's Re-
Creation Day Creme, one Australian woman explained, "I don't know
whether there's a psychological aspect to it or not, but a psychological
reason is as good as any. These creams make you feel good."[17]

This phenomenon is also nothing new. Ginseng for instance, is perhaps the best-known plant in traditional Chinese medicine. Doctors
and patients alike attribute many magical qualities to ginseng roots,
although few of them can be clinically verified. Wild ginseng roots are
typically valued more than domesticated ones, and wild ones shaped
like a man's body can fetch as much as $20,000 an ounce. The high
price is perhaps one of the reasons the legend of ginseng is so persistent
in China. If someone is truly sick and beyond any cure, a traditional
Chinese doctor prescribes the rarest kind of ginseng. If the patient cannot afford it or find it, the doctor absolves himself of any responsibility
for not being able to offer a cure. On the other hand, if the patient man-
ages to get hold of some rare ginseng but does not recover, the family
can still be satisfied that they have tried everything, even the most
expensive remedy money can buy.

Of course, when the patient pays that kind of price, he may actually feel a little better, at least temporarily—if he believes in the magic
plant. Doctors have long known about a placebo effect, the tendency
of patients who believe in a treatment to get better even when the
treatment has no genuine medicinal value. But only in the past few
years have marketers learned that high price alone can have a similar
effect. For example, in a recent study, one group of participants were
given energy drinks that they were told cost $1.89. A second group
was told that although the drink cost $1.89, the school could buy it in
bulk for 89¢. After conducting the test in three different ways, the
scholars concluded that, on average, the participants who drank the
full-price drink finished more puzzles. An earlier study by the same

group found that similar results applied to a gym: Participants who drank the full-priced drink reported more intense workouts, on average, than a second group of discount-drinkers.[18]

Sometimes an expensive product even generates more pleasure than a lower-priced product. Researchers at the California Institute of Technology and Stanford University asked volunteers to try five different Cabernet Sauvignons, each tagged at prices of up to $90 per bottle. In this way, they passed off a $90 bottle of Cabernet Sauvignon as a $10 bottle and presented a $5 bottle as a $45 bottle. They found that not only were the subjects more inclined to rate the allegedly high-priced wines higher than the low-priced wines, but that brain scans confirmed the drinkers actually experienced greater pleasure when they tried the supposedly high-priced vintages. Antonio Rangel, an associate professor of economics at CalTech who worked on the study, concluded that pleasure "seems to depend on our beliefs about our experience of that thing."[19] In other words, by manipulating prices, "we can change how wine tastes without changing the wine," Rangel concluded.[20]

When More Is More

Other companies have also found that high prices help create a perception of quality. Although Microsoft touted the dominance of its operating system for years, Apple executives jealously maintain their niche at the high end of the personal computing market in part by pricing higher than Windows machines and seldom discounting—a high-end strategy, not unlike the strategy of American Express with its black card. "What's wrong with being BMW or Mercedes?" CEO Steve Jobs once asked.

A high price can reassure the client in other ways as well. A medical specialist who demands a high fee provides some reassurance to the patient that his skills command a premium. In psychiatry, Freud went so far as to suggest that the fee was an important part of building an analyst's credibility: He believed that if the patient believed that the psychiatrist's income was at stake, the patient would trust him to provide high-quality service.[21] However, this could be somewhat culturally specific: In France, for instance, professionals who charge a premium relative to the market are often denigrated as people "who work only for money," the implication being that their service is motivated more by a desire for personal profit than by a desire to help the client and may in fact be somewhat less reliable because of it.

The reassuring quality of a high fee might even be a partial explanation for the otherwise puzzling fact that a surprising number of institutional investors don't bother performing any real due diligence on their managers. A recent survey by the Greenwich Roundtable, a nonprofit group that researches alternative investments, found that one in three large institutional investment managers admitted they didn't always run a background check on the fund managers with whom they invested, even though, as fiduciaries, they have a legal responsibility to invest prudently.[22] The high fee evidently led them to let down their guard a bit by identifying fund managers as fellow members of the same professional clan.

Nor does this insight apply only to high-flying professionals. In a way, we all experience the effect of a high fee, or workplace overpaying, if you believe economists Joseph E. Stiglitz and Carl Shapiro.[23] They believe that it's not just the hedge fund managers who are overpaid, but all of us. Their argument is based on the simple observation that unemployment exists in labor markets. To them, the existence of unemployment suggests that employers must be paying a higher-than-market-clearing wage rate. In other words, we are all paid a wage rate that is higher than the wage necessary to induce or secure our labor. For that reason, more labor is supplied than demanded in labor markets. The question Stiglitz and Shapiro asked is, why do employers pay what seems to be an unnecessary high wage?

The answer to that question is the same as in previous examples: The high price or high wage rate serves buyers' (employers') as well as sellers' (employees') economic or psychological interests. In their paper "Equilibrium Unemployment as a Worker Discipline Device," Stiglitz and Shapiro argue that in a perfectly competitive labor market, employers tend to pay more than the absolute rock-bottom wage for a number of reasons. The basic idea is that to induce workers not to shirk their jobs, most firms attempt to pay more than the going wage. When all companies follow suit, however, the higher payroll means that the overall demand for labor decreases, and unemployment results. From the employer's point of view, that unemployment is not a bad thing, according to Stiglitz and Shapiro. It acts as a powerful incentive to work hard. If employees slack off and get fired, they must go back to the pool of the unemployed, where they won't have an easy time matching the same compensation elsewhere. High wages also helps the firm attract the best and brightest workers. If you are the highest-paying employer, everyone in the industry wants to work for you. All other things being equal, you can attract the best people. Thus, the lesson for an employer is that although it's tempting to pay a lower wage rate, because you may still be able to hire the same number of people, you pay for your thrift in the form of lower productivity and less access to talent.

This kind of trade-off is familiar to many marketers, particularly in luxury goods. For consumer goods for which there is no real need to limit production, companies face a constant temptation to lower the price and catch more pent-up demand. This can boost sales in the short run, but in the long run, it can eventually undermine the perceived value of the product.

For this reason, smarter companies that sell high-end products, such as BMW, often make a point of not discounting. Faced with an assertive negotiator, BMW salesmen will sometimes suggest that the consumer "isn't ready" to own a BMW. Even when the product's manufacturing cost is not especially high, high-end marketers often try to set a constant (or rising) price to maintain a high perceived value of the product's quality. For example, American Girl, a division of Mattel, never discounts its core products, high-quality 18-inch dolls. Mattel sells every doll for $95, despite the fact that some models must sell more than others. Slow-movers are discontinued instead of discounted, creating scarcity and increasing the value of the doll among collectors in the after-market.

Apple Computer is one of the experts in this kind of pricing. As we mentioned earlier, it's one of the few electronics companies that has tried to avoid a low-priced commodity strategy. The iPhone is a case in point. When Apple's iPhone was introduced to the market, it was priced far higher than other phones. This was no surprise: Most electronics products for which there is strong demand charge more for early adopters. However, Apple did not take the usual course consumer electronics follows of repricing down the demand curve as it exhausts prospects. Instead, after an initial repricing, Apple added new features to maintain the high cost—and the mystique. Other Apple products have maintained the same pricing structure. With the iPod, for instance, the price has remained high, but new features keep being added to maintain the consumer's perception of value. To capture the more price-conscious segment of the market, the company introduced a different product, the Nano, with a more limited feature set, including less storage space.

Sometimes companies attempt to not only set the current price, but try to find ways to set a floor on future prices. For example, Mattel's fixed price helps the company communicate to parents and grandparents the idea that its American Girl dolls are not a fashion-driven item, but a high-value toy that their daughters and granddaughters will play with for years. By contrast, Barbie dolls, Mattel's biggest-selling line of dolls, are more fashion driven and sold at a variety of price points.

Sometimes companies also try to influence the secondary market as a way to maintain a high price. The makers of expensive Swiss watches, for example, have been very active in bidding up the prices of old watches to encourage customers to believe that luxury watches have investment value. Stories about record-setting prices enable the customer to see their purchase of an expensive watch less as a luxury good than as an investment that will hold its value over time. For example, following a high-profile auction of an old Omega watch for $351,000, a 1950s platinum watch at a 2007 auction by "a Swiss bidder" (Omega itself, a fact the company left out of its publicity), Seattle retailer Steven Goldfarb noted that although prior to the publicity around the sale he had sold mostly $1,400 models, now he was selling models costing three times that figure. "Customers are conscious of the fact that an Omega watch sold for $300,000," he says. "They have no idea who bought it."[24]

As problematic as this strategy might be for the company's credibility in the long run, in the short run it does appear to be a good way to keep prices up. By contrast, a flexible pricing policy for luxury goods often leads to terrible results. In the automobile industry, flexibility on price has helped destroy the perceived value of a number of high-end brands. For years, American luxury cars competed on price against foreign cars that refused to play the game, a process that ultimately helped destroy some formerly strong brands, such as Cadillac. Although many other factors, particularly quality and costs, contributed to Detroit's loss of power, price promotions must have helped accelerate the hollowing out of the American luxury marks' perceived value.

This often happens in consumer goods as well. Motorola's Razr phones, for instance, went from being a "must-have" fashion accessory to just another cell phone, largely because of excessive discounting.

Done wrong, discounting of prices that had some expressive value can even lead to wholesale destruction not just of a brand, but of an entire class of products. For example, Saks Fifth Avenue's price-slashing sales in November 2008 (ahead of the usual post-Christmas sales) may have kept the department store alive through the downturn, but Saks' survival strategy came at the expense of most of its vendors. A number of vendors believe that the 70% off sales destroyed the value of luxury goods permanently. Indeed, some shoppers said they would refuse to pay full price in the future. "I am so shocked that I ever did pay full price," said Roz Silbershatz, a 29-year-old communications executive. "I could never do that again."[25]

When Less Is More

Edward Filene's prophecy that the "the businessman of the future, whether manufacturer or merchant, will make more money by reducing prices than the businessman of the past ever made by raising them"[26] may have been fulfilled by some of the world's most successful retailers. But it's not always true. There are plenty of reasons why a company may want to charge high prices or even abnormally high prices. High prices can screen customers, signal value and quality of a product or service, motivate employees, and nurture customer loyalty, depending on where and how you charge them. However, it is important to note that a high price isn't the only kind of price that can add value to a product. In some situations, extremely low prices can perform these functions and add expressive values as well—sometimes even in financial services.

In 1974, the Securities and Exchange Commission began deregulating stock commissions. Some brokers, such as Bear Sterns, lowered commissions as of May 1. Three-hundred-pound gorilla Merrill Lynch actually used its newfound freedom to raise its commissions 3%, unaware of how much the world had changed.[27]

Chuck Schwab of Charles Schwab & Co. capitalized on the opportunity. He caught the high-margin industry off guard with discount commissions that undercut the traditional brokerage houses by 80%. He backed the low price with another pricing innovation as well: Orders were all taken by salaried brokers who had no incentive to buy or sell any particular stocks or to trade more often than the client wanted, a frequent source of client complaint in traditional, commission-driven brokerage houses.[28]

In time, Schwab's model became one of the dominant designs in the industry. Many of today's brokers—now restyled as financial advisors—have also changed their pricing. Even the full-service brokerage houses have tried to move many employees if not to cheaper pricing, then to simpler pricing, charging on a percentage of assets basis instead of by trade, which they argue eliminates a conflict of interest.

Other kinds of service companies have also found ways to turn low price into an expressive benefit. NetFlix transformed its industry in part through a simple, low-price structure. Before NetFlix, rental companies such as Blockbuster made substantial amounts of revenue on differential pricing between new releases and old movies, as well as late fees for movies not returned on time. NetFlix offers a simple subscription plan that treats all releases the same and includes no late fees. The tardy subscriber's only punishment is that the company does not send another movie until the borrowed title is returned.

The NetFlix model worked partly because of advances in technology. The shift from video to DVD made shipping movies feasible and reduced the storage costs of holding multiple copies. The Internet also made it possible to maintain a vast online catalog, while saving money on a physical storefront. A modern distribution center and a simple return envelope completed the system operationally. However, it would not have been nearly as successful without the simple subscription and no-late-fee pricing plan. This pricing format made DVD watching feel free, since the subscription became a fixed cost, similar to a cable subscription, that customers need not think about until the credit card bill arrived—and, even then, might overlook. As with Amazon's Subscribe & Save Program (discussed in Chapter 7,

"Subscribe and Save: Pricing for Marketing Profitability"), NetFlix's subscription model transformed the movie-watching habits of millions from an impulse buy on the way home to a regular event.

Low prices can generate loyalty in other ways as well. In New York, the same city where Trump used a high price to create a sense of distinction, some restaurants use relatively low prices and a policy of not taking reservations to create a high degree of loyalty. John's Pizza is one such restaurant. At John's, lines often stretch outside. The pizza is good and affordable, a rare combination in New York. And because John's takes no reservations, yet is a pleasant place to eat, the restaurant often has a line. Creating this kind of broad-based devotion can also help create a customer base that is presumably less fickle than high-end diners—and probably just as loyal during an economic downturn as a boom.

Rock concert promoters sometimes price tickets in similar ways. On local television, photos of young people camping out for days before a show are such a staple that no one questions why such lines should exist. Why wouldn't the sponsors of the show just raise the price until the market clears and no one has to wait? Or, in that other common news story—the show that sells out in minutes—why wouldn't the promoters raise the price so they met the demand of only the highest-price segment of the market? The answer is that underpricing helps create more awareness for the show—and, by extension, awareness of the band itself and demand for the band's other products.

Besides building the customer base, low prices can help screen customers and create a devoted audience. That's the real reason some popular shows and sporting events often sell a certain number of cheaper seats. Having younger and perhaps more passionate people out front can add a different energy level to the TV and stadium audience than might be present if everyone in the stands paid top dollar.

In New York again, that city of pricing extremes, some of the most popular shows are the Shakespeare in the Park performances in the summer. The plays are popular in part because movie stars often take roles. But they are also popular because of a certain kind of artificial scarcity created by their pricing. The tickets are not sold ahead of time—in fact, they are not sold at all. Instead, the tickets are given away. Paradoxically, this makes Shakespeare in the Park the most expensive ticket in town for a working person: To get a ticket, one must be willing to line up early in the morning and wait for five or six hours until the tickets are distributed at 11 a.m.—a huge financial investment at any level of income.

Giving away the tickets began as an act of cultural philanthropy by Public Theater impresario Joseph Papp, but 50 seasons of Shakespeare in the Park suggest that a workable business model must be lurking in the shadows. For the nonprofit Public Theater, which produces the program, the no-price shows pay off in three ways. First, the lines and the full houses have built a broad awareness of the Public and its programs. Second, the lines set a high perceived value for tickets that are "given" to corporate sponsors. Finally, the free shows are seen by 100,000 appreciative theatergoers every season, an audience that corporate sponsors find desirable.

Shakespeare might have been right that a rose by any other name would smell as sweet, but we may add, not by any other price. If roses were the cheapest among all flowers, they almost certainly would not have become lovers' favorites anymore than gold or diamonds would have been the top choices for rings. As all the examples in this chapter suggest, price alone can be an important element in generating not only economic value, but also expressive value. Whether that price is extraordinarily high or extraordinarily low—a $39 burger at the Four Seasons in New York or a free play in Central Park—the price itself is part of what creates the subsequent experience.

Endnotes

[1]Schmith, Scott, "Credit Card Market: Economic Benefits and Industry Trends," International Trade Administration, U.S. Department of Commerce, (March 2008): 4.

[2]Thornton, Emily, "Fees, Fees, Fees!", *BusinessWeek* (September 29, 2003): 98.

[3]CNN Money.com, July 18, 2007.

[4]Wainright, Martin, "Royal Bank Launches Super Premium Plastic," *The Guardian* (23 November 2004): http://www.guardian.co.uk/money/2004/nov/23/creditcards.debt.

[5]Financial Planning's SMA Advisor newsletter (December 2004).

[6]Navone, Marco A., Belleri, Matteao, "Hedge Funds: Ability, Persistence, and Style," Carefin Research Paper No 8/08 (July 31, 2008).

[7]Ibid.

[8]Hulburt, Mark, "2+20, the Other Hedge Fund Math," *The New York Times* (March 4, 2007): http://www.nytimes.com/2007/03/04/business/yourmoney/04stra.html.

[9]McDonald, Duff, "The Running of the Hedge Hogs,: New York Magazine (April 9, 2007).

[10]Owen, James, P., *The Prudent Investor's Guide to Hedge Funds* (New York: John Wiley & Sons, 2000), 54.

[11]Brown, Stephen, *Hedge Funds: Omniscient or Just Plain Wrong* (New York: New York University, 2001), 5.

[12]Litt, Michael, *Prudence: Paradigm Shift in Pension & Wealth Management* Washington, D.C.: American Enterprise Institute, 2006).

[13]Brooks, John, *The Go-Go Years* (New York: John Wiley & Sons, 1999).

[14]Eichengreen, Barry J., et. al., *"Hedge Funds and Financial Market Dynamics"* Volume 166 of Occasional Papers of the International Monetary Fund (Washington, D.C.: International Monetary Fund, 1998).

[15]Statman, Meir "What do Investors Want?" *Journal of Portfolio Management* (2004): 153–160.

[16]Tuccille, Jerome, *Trump: The Saga of America's Most Powerful Real Estate Baron* (Washington, DC: Beard Books, 2004).

[17]Hughes, Natasha, "Women Rush Tiny Tubs of Rolled Gold Crème," *Sunday Age* (May 6, 2007): 8.

[18]Arielly, Dan, et al.,"Placebo Effects of Marketing Actions," *Journal of Marketing Research* (2005): 383.

[19]Dunleavey, M.P., "My Cortex Made Me Buy It," *New York Times* (February 9, 2008).

[20]Gellene, Denise, "Why We Like Pricey Wines," *Los Angeles Times* (January 15, 2008).

[21]Winter, Sarah, *Freud and the Institution of Psychoanalytic Knowledge* (Palo Alto: Stanford University Press, 1999): 140.

[22]Zweig, Jason, "How Bernie Madoff Made Smart Folks Look Dumb," *Wall Street Journal* (December 13, 2008).

[23]Shapiro, Carl and Joseph Stiglitz, "Equilibrium Unemployment as a Worker Discipline Device," *American Economic Review* 74 (no. 3), June 1984: 433-444.

[24]Meichtry, Stacy, "Invisible Hand: How Top Watchmakers Intervene in Auctions: Luxury Time Pieces Get Pumped Up in Bidding," *Wall Street Journal* (October 8, 2007): A1.

[25]O'Connell, Vanessa and Dodes, Rachel, "Saks Upends Luxury Market with Strategy to Slash Prices," *Wall Street Journal* (February 9, 2009).

[26]Berkeley, George E., *The Filenes* (Wellesley, Mass.: Branden Books, 1998): 190.

[27]Kador, John, Charles Schwab: How one company beat Wall Street and reinvented the brokerage industry (New York: Wiley, 2002): 25.

[28]Ibid., 42.

9

Pay If It Works

"Half the money I spend on advertising is wasted; the trouble is, I don't know which half."
John Wanamaker, department store owner

In the century since Philadelphia retail pioneer John Wanamaker made his famous quip about wasted advertising money, a lot has changed in the world. But one thing has remained the same: Vendors still spend billions on advertising and other services and products without knowing for sure whether they have wasted their money until after they have spent it—an incredible fact that makes many transactions not all that different from the story of Jack trading the cow for some magic beans.

This is changing now, however, partly because of advances in technology and partly because of an innovative new pricing practice: performance-based pricing. From advertising to pharmaceuticals, from consulting to construction, from health care to manufacturing, companies are increasingly moving to a "pay if it works" pricing model—a radical shift in strategy that promises to change many buyer and seller relationships forever.

Traditionally, most purchases are the outcome of a conflict. The seller always wants the buyer to pay more; the buyer always wants to pay less. When a transaction occurs, the two sides have normally reached some sort of compromise. Unless one side is all-powerful—such as in a monopoly—neither is completely happy about the conclusion of this zero-sum game: A penny less in price makes the buyer a penny richer and the seller a penny poorer.

Some markets are happier than others. Not long ago, pharmaceutical companies tended to bring home more of what they wanted, and consumers were happy enough to pay. A drug that makes someone's life better—and sometimes even saves it—is about as compelling as a value proposition can get. But in the last decade, customers have grown more restive. Prices have risen far faster than inflation. In the United States alone, prescription drug sales grew from $216.7 billion in 2006 to $274.9 billion in 2007.[1] Not coincidentally, the industry has slipped from being one of the most admired industries in the United States to one of the most despised. Big Pharma now ranks right up with Big Tobacco as an industry that people love to hate.[2] John Le Carre, the spy novelist who made his name writing Cold War stories, even wrote a thriller, *The Constant Gardener* (2001), in which Big Pharma played the villain.

Pharmaceutical companies argue that prices have risen because their costs have risen. Drug-development costs are 15 times higher than they were in the 1970s and three times higher than they were in the 1980s.[3] Today bringing a new product to market costs an average of $1.1 billion and takes roughly 12.5 years, according to John Patterson, the director of development at AstraZeneca.[4] Inventing winning compounds is also more difficult. In 2007, the Food and Drug Administration approved just 19 new drugs, the lowest number in 20 years. The low yield was blamed partly on the fact that the nature of the scientific challenge is more complex and partly on rising costs, which have led regulators to ask tougher questions now about the therapeutic value of the new entry. It's no longer enough for a drug to be a unique formula; to win approval, the drug must be demonstrably better than any existing drug it replaces and create some additional new economic or therapeutic value for the patient. With so many hoops, only one in 5,000 compounds makes it to the market.[5]

To make matters worse, the pharmaceutical company also has less time to recoup its development costs. Longer development times and a shorter term of patent protection have reduced the average post-launch period in which the company can recoup its costs to only 8 years, down from the 12 years companies enjoyed as recently as 2001. Forced to recoup its investment in one-third less time, the drug developer inevitably tries to set a much higher price for its compound.

Advances in genetic knowledge have also meant that more drugs are targeted to narrower groups of patients. An increasing number of drugs are good for only a particular segment of the population. Such specialization is helping make payers more reluctant to pay for the misses, especially when the payers are government institutions or big insurance companies.

For all these reasons, the chances that a compound is successful have dropped dramatically. Alan Sheppard, a consultant at health consultancy IMS Health, estimates that the odds of a new drug becoming a blockbuster (a drug that creates more than a $1 billion market) have dropped in half during the past decade, from 10 to 1 to 20 to 1.[6]

But the public is increasingly unsympathetic. Although consumers are still buying plenty of drugs, they no longer buy Pharma's argument about why drugs must be expensive. In the United States—a relatively less price-regulated market—an alliance of consumers, government payers, and managed care providers are fighting to rein in drug costs. The transactions between consumers and buyers have become so heated that politicians have taken note. The federal government now seems likely to take a leading role in fixing drug prices, an event that now seems inevitable to many in the industry.

The big picture is that Big Pharma wants to charge a high price, but its customers want to pay a low price. In the end, someone will blink. Or will they? We believe that by taking performance-based payments, the industry could sidestep this conflict and create a new working arrangement that leaves patients, payers, and the drug producers themselves all happier than they are right now.

We're optimistic because advanced drugs are essentially intellectual property. Unlike the $20,000-an-ounce rare ginseng root that we mentioned in Chapter 8, "The Snob Premium," the value of the actual physical compound is a relatively small part of the drug's overall cost. These days, the pill itself might almost be thought of as a specialized kind of CD-ROM. As with a number of other innovative pricing strategies we have looked at in this book, understanding that the real value is not the pill, but the intellectual property behind the pill, opens up many new possibilities for pricing. Although companies are now experimenting with a variety of models, including attempts to charge by subscriptions instead of by the physical unit, we believe the model with the most possibility for solving the industry's pricing problem is "pay if it works."

A Focus on Value

Pharmaceutical companies in Canada began experimenting with performance-based pricing in the mid-1990s, but only recently have such moves gained any international traction.[7] Perhaps the best-known pay-for-value player is Johnson & Johnson (J&J), which began marketing a new cancer drug in the United Kingdom in 2007.

Johnson & Johnson's foray began as an innovative counterproposal. J&J had proposed Velcade as a treatment for multiple myeloma, a kind of incurable bone cancer, but the National Institute for Health and Clinical Excellence (NICE), which provides advisory support on drug sales to Britain's national health system, ruled that prescribing the drug would be a waste of the government's money. The drug is priced at £3,000 ($4,500) per treatment cycle but is not entirely reliable.[8] After the rebuff, Janssen–Cilag, the subsidiary of Johnson & Johnson handling the introduction of the drug to the market, countered with a novel offer: a full refund for any patient who didn't experience a 25% reduction in the paraproteins produced by the cancer after four rounds of treatment.

For the patient or the patient's insurer, this proposition seemed hard to refuse. The patient got a chance to try an expensive treatment without the risk of wasting money. And regulators liked it because the National Health Service wouldn't be stuck paying for an ineffective drug. The strategy also wouldn't create any perverse incentives to not improve the drug, as could easily happen if the price had been fixed. "Pay if it works" pricing serves to "focus innovation and investment on the areas where patients need it most, creating more valuable drugs in the future,"[9] in the words of John Fingleton, CEO of the United Kingdom's Office of Fair Trading.

For the pharma company, "pay if it works" might sound risky, but it actually accomplishes three goals. First, it turns a payer's "no" into a "maybe." Second, "pay if it works" overcomes the Wanamakerian objection that under conventional pricing strategies, drugs that don't work still need to be paid for. Third, it turns the discussion away from the inherently defensive debate over whether a price is justified and redirects the debate toward the more positive—and winnable— debate over how much value the drug has created.

Beyond the marketing benefit of being perceived as a company that stands behind its product, "pay if it works" puts a company in a good position to charge a premium to compensate for its earlier risks. Instead of naming a cost-plus price based on how much the company spent on development, the company can name a price based on the value created. For example, in the case of Velcade, rather than wrangle with U.K. health regulators over what the correct price should be, based on the costs of other drugs and the company's development costs, Johnson & Johnson successfully shifted the debate to how much more cost-effective taking Velcade was compared to previous treatments.

"Pay if it works" seems to work particularly well when the pharma company is negotiating with an institutional payer. For example, Pfizer made a recent deal with the state of Florida, offering to return part of the cost of certain Pfizer drugs reimbursed by the state's Medicaid program if the drugs didn't save the state money on its overall health bill, as monitored by an independent auditor. The perform-ance-based approach worked: Pfizer saved the state $41.9 million and eliminated the need for Pfizer to offer a discount or a rebate to con-vince the state of the drug's value.[10]

Reframed in this way, the value proposition of a new drug becomes extremely compelling. As one industry consultant puts it, "What's a product or service that will help you live longer with better quality of life worth to you?"[11] Expensive as pharmaceuticals are, they are often much cheaper than the alternative, whether it is suffering or more invasive—and sometimes less effective—physical treatments. A 2002 study found that every dollar spent on the newer pharmaceuti-cals resulted in a savings of $6.17 in total health-care spending.[12]

Given all these benefits, it's not surprising that Pharma isn't the only part of the health care sector that now uses "pay if it works" con-tracts. Fertility clinics, for example, often use performance-based pricing. This plan seems likely to catch on elsewhere, too, as regula-tors push physicians to prescribe treatments based on empirical results—an idea that drives health-care providers straight toward a "pay if it works" strategy. To try to cope with skyrocketing medical costs, many policy wonks in Washington and, more importantly, policymakers in the Obama administration, believe that adopting an evidence-based health-care system could be an important way for the country to save money while improving the quality of care. One Con-gressional Budget Office expert estimates that less than 50% of all medical treatments have been demonstrated to be effective and argues that weeding out useless treatments could be an important way to reduce the country's health-care bills.[13] Policymakers see this idea as so promising that the Obama administration earmarked $1.1 billion in its first budget to underwrite federal efforts to compile data on the relative effectiveness of different health-care treatments.[14] In such a political environment, "pay if it works" begins to seem not only like a good pricing option, but for expensive, uncertain treatments, maybe the only one.

"Pay if it works" is also finding its way into a number of other industries that once had pricing problems. Software has had some luck with "pay if it works" schemes. Honeywell, for example, ties payment for its heating and cooling building control systems to the building's energy cost savings.[15] Pay if it works has proven so successful in fact that some Indian business process outsourcing companies have reportedly begun to emulate the practice.[16] Looking forward, Forrester Research argues that "pay if it works" will become a norm in IT. "As outsourcing matures, IT managers are looking for value and a more defined business impact from their outsourcing relationships," analysts write. One way to drive that kind of longer-term thinking is to change compensation so that it rewards not what the contractor put into the work, but what the client company got out of it.

Duncan Aitchison, managing director of TPI, a sourcing advisory firm, agrees.[17] "As contracts mature and service providers demonstrate their capabilities, more sophisticated outcome-based pricing might be tied to the vendor's ability to provide productivity improvements," he says.

In other kinds of industrial automation, some industry gurus are even arguing that this kind of pricing structure may be the only way for high-cost service companies to compete in the global economy. Consultant Jim Pinto argues that in a world where Chinese companies are happy to take home gross margins of 5–10%, the only chance automation vendors have to serve their customers is to reinvent their pricing structure and sell what truly matters to their customers: performance.[18]

Nontechnical industries are even finding uses for "pay if it works." Advertising agencies during the last two decades have traded away their traditional structures of 15% of billings fee in favor of more performance-based pricing for their creative work.[19] Now advertising itself appears to be moving even further, with an innovation that Wanamaker would certainly have approved of. Google's keywords program and other online programs are not only making the ineffective "half" of advertising increasingly clear, but they are asking their clients to pay for only the effective half. In online advertising especially, performance-based pricing now seems to be squeezing out the price-per-impression model that was standard in the first years of the Internet. In 2006, the two models were almost equally popular, but now the cost per thousand (CPM) model pulls just 39% of all online revenue, even as performance-based contracts brought home almost 57%.[20]

Consultants are also now experimenting with the new model, particularly those who sell technical and operational advice. *The Wall Street Journal* reported that a 2006 survey found that although performance-based pricing is still rare among consultants—a survey of 218 top U.S. firms found that less than 5% of engagements are set on a performance basis—the practice is growing rapidly.[21] Already some giants in the industry, particularly advisors on information systems installation, such as Accenture and IBM, sometimes make their compensation contingent on the success of their plan, paid through a share of the upside of any cost savings or sales gains their work helps generate.

Performance-based pricing is not without risks for the seller, but in certain contexts, it can be an important tool. As we have seen, performance-based pricing can even create sales when the buyer's concerns about cost-effectiveness might otherwise be a deal breaker. It also has at least three other important advantages.

Performance-based pricing aligns the interests of buyers and sellers

"Pay if it works" removes the buyer's biggest objection: Reframing the price reduces the up-front risk on the buyer's side and makes the buyer more willing to enter into the agreement. As with a money-back guarantee on a consumer good, a performance-based price helps encourage the customer to give the product a try.[22] For the seller, "pay if it works" entails taking on a lot more risk. However, it also creates the potential for greater rewards.[23]

Nor is this true only for pharma. As novel as "pay if it works" pricing is in most contexts, some professionals have worked on a pay-for-performance basis for many years. Personal injury lawyers, for example, have long received 30%–40% of any settlement, usually in lieu of an hourly fee. In the United States, the practice is long-established—such options have been around for at least a century.[24]

Legal scholars say the "pay if it works" structure helps avoid some conflicts of interest that can occur in kinds of law where by-the-hour work is more common. People might balk at paying one-third of their settlement to the lawyer, but the fact that personal injury attorneys receive one-third means that the lawyer's share can never exceed the size of the settlement, which might otherwise be the case.

On the defense side of personal injury suits, the rule of thumb is $1 in legal costs for every $1 paid in a settlement.[25] In other branches of the law, by-the-hour costs sometimes even exceed the entire sum at risk. Hourly attorneys, for example, have long been criticized for allegedly running up the meter during bankruptcy proceedings—sometimes so much so that no assets remain for the creditors they are ostensibly serving. And in situations when two hourly attorneys meet, the incentives are largely on the side of complexity.

This conflict is so common that it has been the stuff of black comedy for at least 150 years, such as the long-running suit that propels the plot of Charles Dickens's novel, *Bleak House*: "The little plaintiff or defendant who was promised a new rocking horse when Jarndyce and Jarndyce should be settled has grown up, possessed himself of a real horse, and trotted away into the other world."

Performance-based pricing takes lawyers and their clients into a better world because both sides work as effectively as possible to maximize the pie they will eventually share. This incentive alignment makes it easier for both sides to work with each other even during a long litigation and settlement process. It also encourages them to engage in a more free and frank exchange of information as they both work for that bigger pie.

Other kinds of transaction-oriented professional services have also been compensated on a "pay if it works" basis for this same reason. Real estate agents receive a 6% or 7% commission on the selling price of property they sell. Literary agents receive 15%. Hedge fund managers—at least until the recent crash—earned 2% of assets and 20% of the gains. Investment banks typically receive 7% of realized IPO value when they prepare and underwrite a company's IPO. This arrangement seems common in situations where the client finds it difficult to monitor the time and effort of the service provider but needs to ensure that the provider's interests are aligned with his own.

Performance-based pricing tends to reduce competition on price

There is no intrinsic reason why lawyers should get one-third of a settlement or real estate agents should receive 6%–7%, but when such conventions take hold, they tend to become an unquestioned feature of the industry and, typically, the base price. When the price is set, firms compete on everything but their rate, which becomes somehow sacrosanct. This stability arises for a few reasons. First, in professional services, potential clients might view a low price as a sign of low quality. In addition, because many professional services are not scalable businesses, discounts can't be made up in volume, and a provider has less incentive to lower the rate. Second, the client might not want to negotiate a lower rate. If the service provider accepts an offer inferior to the industry standard, the reflective client might not sleep well, thinking that the service provider might not put in the right level of time and effort on the client's behalf. If the rate for one client's case is lower but the professional is charging others more, where will the service provider spend his time if a time conflict arises? Finally, many industries in which "pay if it works" pricing prevails have cartel-like characteristics. Members could collectively punish someone who tried to compete on price, such as by excluding them from a share of a large deal or by locking them out of mutual-defense arrangements during a tough time.

Performance-based pricing acts as a kind of insurance against undercharging or overpaying

From the seller's point of view, it is more difficult for the customer to object to a price after the vendor has created some positive value. An executive is much more likely to make room in a budget for a percentage of hypothetical gains made through projected cost savings than an up-front cost that promises savings next year: *Show me the beanstalk, and then we'll talk.* If the product or service performs well, the buyer will not stint on payment. By the same token, such an agreement protects the buyer against overpayment. In essence, such a pricing structure protects buyers against downside risk, while compensating vendors by giving them a share in the upside—a risk balance that can create mutual benefit if the product is effective.

Performance-based pricing can improve price segmentation

"Pay if it works" acts as insurance in another way, too, by avoiding heterogeneity problems—that is, the problem of how to extract different prices from different customers. Essentially, as Thomas Nagle of the Monitor Group puts it in describing one kind of performance-pay drug program, "pay if it works" is a strategy that "enables the company to give a discount when payers allow the drug to be used in populations with a high risk of failure, while still enabling the company to capture full value from populations where failures are less likely."[26]

Performance-based pricing improves deals

Payment on performance means that the buyer and seller must define success in an extremely clear way. This process of sitting down to define success is an important ancillary benefit to a performance-based pricing structure. Such a process often uncovers new opportunities to cut costs or create more value. In fact, Harvard professor Benson Shapiro argues that the necessity for more communication is really one of the most important advantages of performance-based pricing.[27] We agree.

For example, pay-for-performance pricing helps avoid the kind of channel conflict we call double-marginalization, in which the combined margins of the retailer and the wholesale manufacturer are so high that they depress consumer demand for the product. In 1997, for example, executives at Blockbuster Video realized that video retailers were all losing sales because they could not afford to stock enough copies of the latest releases to satisfy demand. As Sumner Redstone, chairman of Viacom, later recalled, "The whole business was operating wrong ... there weren't enough tapes in the stores.... Year after year, the studios kept raising the price of tapes to companies like Blockbuster. When the price of tapes got up to about $65 each, we realized we couldn't afford to buy enough tapes to sufficiently stock the shelves."[28]

Viacom's Blockbuster unit asked for steeper discounts, but the studios turned down the company because they had their own interests to look after. Why shouldn't they maximize the gains on their own intellectual property? The reason, Blockbuster argued, was that by using a new pricing arrangement, the two could make more money working together than they could separately. Blockbuster proposed a new arrangement to Disney with lower up-front costs per video but with a revenue share. In the end, Disney saw the logic and agreed to accept $7 a video, the price of the video on the secondary market, plus 40% of the return on each rental. This new agreement enabled Blockbuster to stock 100 tapes of a hit movie in a given outlet instead of 30, making it possible for Blockbuster to rent the movie to virtually everyone who wanted to see it in the first few days of release, not just the customers who got to the video store early. The strategy worked well—U.S. market share for Blockbuster grew from 28% to 41% between 1997 and 2001. The end result: "Blockbuster's happy, the studios are happy, and consumers are happy because they get what they want," Redstone later recalled. Blockbuster's new arrangement worked so well that the other studios soon followed suit.

Making "Pay If It Works" Work

But performance-based pricing isn't for everyone. Five conditions seem particularly necessary to make this kind of pricing succeed:

The outcome must be verifiable

Success in "pay if it works" pricing must be both measurable and verifiable. Measurable in the sense that the gains are quantitative: The patient got better and recovery can be shown, such as in the growth of red blood cells. The beanstalk actually does reach to the sky. *Verifiable* in that the vendor can quantitatively demonstrate success: *Follow me and I'll show you the giant's castle.* "Pay if it works" is probably not a good strategy in a qualitative business. For example, art dealers often work on a "pay if it works" basis with its artists (typically a 50% commission on sale), but "pay if it works" won't work for buyers.

Even when the outcome can be clearly measured, it's important to decide in advance who will do the measuring. For example, the Disney–Blockbuster deal mentioned previously foundered after Disney alleged that Blockbuster hadn't lived up to its end of the bargain. After several years of successful performance-based collaboration on video rentals and sales, Disney sued Blockbuster in 2002 for selling its videos sooner than agreed and for not marketing the videos sufficiently—breaches that Disney claimed cost the company $120 million in lost revenue.[29] This measurement issue is perhaps the biggest reason pay-for-performance tends not to work well for longer-term complex contracts or a sale in which there is no single quantifiable outcome.

The transaction focuses on particular objectives, not the client's overall success

"Pay if it works" tends to succeed more often if the project in question is of limited scope, such as with the sale of a house or the installation of a new IT system that can save the client money in a very quantifiable way. The vendor typically ensures that it isn't taking on a lot of risk outside its control. For example, maintenance tends to be an important part of agreements involving a complex machine or system.

Without this limitation, open-ended risk sharing can be quite problematic. During the dotcom boom for example, many lawyers and consultants traded their services for stock, which would be valuable if the company they advised succeeded. After many of those companies fell apart—not necessarily because of any bad advice the firms gave—some of those service firms also failed. Brobeck, Phleger & Harrison, a leading San Francisco law firm during the dotcom era, was one notable casualty. Normally, corporate law firms are close to indestructible. Fees are paid on an ongoing basis, partners' pay is a variable cost (based largely on the individual's performance), and downturns in business are usually handled by shrinking the firm (typically by laying off associates and trimming office space).[30]

However, Brobeck often took stock instead of cash. This sounded like a good idea when the market was creating dozens of overnight billionaires, but when the stock market went south, so did Brobeck.

Failure would not destroy the seller

As the Brobeck case suggests, pay-for-performance is not a good model for a company serving a relatively concentrated industry or a single client. This may also create some complex revenue-recognition issues that could end up making the deal more of a boon for the seller's accountant than for the seller.[31] Start-ups with cash flow issues may also want to think twice before entering into such an arrangement. In such a case, a mix of up-front and performance pricing would probably be more appropriate.

Over-concentrated portfolios can create problems for clients as well. Vendors betting too much on too few deals may run into cash flow issues. In contrast, a vendor with a broad base of pay-for-performance cases might be an advantage for the client. A broad base helps ensure that the vendor has a steady business, and it might increase the client's value as a third-party advisor. For example, personal injury lawyers, who typically manage a number of cases at the same time, argue that their portfolio of cases mirrors those of the insurance companies (who are the true defendant in most injury cases), making it easier for them to negotiate a settlement with more objectivity than if clients tried to negotiate on their own.[32]

The outcome is valuable to both parties

The outcome of the agreement must also be of substantial interest to the client and much greater than the price of the sale.

"Pay if it works" transactions typically arise when the buyer has a significant interest in the potential gain. Such "skin in the game" is important because the success of most services sold in this way requires some level of cooperation from the user, even if the product or service costs nothing up front. A share of a future benefit keeps both sides interested in the outcome in a way that a fixed price at the finish line would not.

In the case of real estate, Saul Levmore, dean of the University of Chicago Law School, has speculated about why agents work on a 6% commission instead of simply what he calls a "100% commission"—the right to skim any profits if the home sells beyond a certain price. The reason, he speculates, is that a percentage deal keeps the client interested in the outcome, and the client's cooperation is important to maximize the value of the sale. "With a 100% commission in place, agents would need to contract for such things as property maintenance, appropriate behavior by principals when potential buyers explore the property, and so forth," he speculates.[33]

From Adversary to Partner

Ultimately, "pay if it works" pricing is unique because it transforms each transaction into a partnership. All businesses rely on their customers, but performance-based pricing makes that relationship even clearer. By putting their money where their mouth is, vendors who use "pay if it works" pricing send a powerful statement about the value of their service and the value they place on their customers' success.

The sales proposition becomes so compelling in fact that, in industries where it takes hold, it tends to squeeze out other models. Sometimes there can even be knock-on effects in closely related industries when such a shift occurs: Even as advertising has adapted itself to more payment on performance, old-line media companies that are accustomed to profit from the less quantifiable kind of advertising models continue to suffer.

Perhaps they, too, will need to reinvent their model. Theoretically, it could be done. One classic *Wall Street Journal* direct-mail advertisement that has run for decades is a letter that tells the story of two men who meet 20 years after their graduation. The story contrasts a man who read the *Wall Street Journal* diligently from the beginning of his career and one who didn't. The moral of the sales letter, of course, is that the better-informed individual has had the better career—implying that a *Wall Street Journal* subscription is a valuable personal investment.

Assuming that reading the *Wall Street Journal* really is this valuable, how much would that subscription be worth to the more successful reader? Quite a lot, probably. But although paying a newspaper subscription retroactively is not possible because the value is difficult to demonstrate, other information providers could make analogous propositions. For example, why couldn't higher education—which often has a high rate of return, particularly in professional education—be paid for by 1% of income for life, instead of by tuition?

Such a plan would have some advantages (and not only for Wharton, which would be able to claim retroactive tuition from Warren Buffett for the time he spent there!). More students would apply, undeterred by the cost and fear of educational loans, creating a stronger student body. Students would choose their schools, studies, and careers based on their interests and talents, not out of concern about their ability to pay off their loans. Over time, those who gained more in monetary terms from their education would pay more in financial terms—and because most degrees create financial value for students, the long-run returns for the university might be much greater than the short-run cost of tuition. Eventually, schools would have even more of an incentive to offer good students scholarships: They would want to cast the net wide to catch the likes of a Buffett or his bridge partner, Bill Gates. They might even want to work harder to keep students like Buffett and Gates from moving elsewhere or dropping out.

The only real difficulty would be verifying income. If income could be verified—and with a little government cooperation, it could be—the 1% solution might be a better model than the current complex mess of loans and aid. Nor is this quite as far-fetched as it sounds. The U.S. state and federal governments already do this with children's services, essentially, through the income tax code. Heavy investments are made in these future taxpayers' health and education, which they then repay later when they begin paying into the system. In a way, the history of the GI Bill is a good example of the potential value of "pay if it works" financing.

In the future, we expect that changes in society and in technology will make "pay if it works" even more attractive. Just as some past pricing strategies in many industries grew out of technological improvements—airline yield management wouldn't have gotten far without computers—so too will "pay if it works."

We're also confident about "pay if it works" pricing because it follows the same trend we have seen throughout this book, in everything from pharmaceuticals, to computers, to music: a movement away from hide-bound industry pricing conventions toward pricing that is flexible, targeted, and customer-oriented.

Today more marketers are learning that companies can price a product or service in many different ways and that some are much better for particular applications than others. Over all, pricing methods that prey on the buyer's ignorance are on their way out, while pricing methods that treat customers as knowledgeable partners, such as "pay if it works," are in. Some of these innovative methods, such as "pay if it works" or "pay as you wish," take us full circle—back to the bazaar, to the kind of individual, customer-by-customer haggling that was once scarcely different from conversation but that grew over time into modern mass-market retailing. As the capability to monitor performance in pharmaceuticals and other sectors continues to improve, it seems likely that an increasing number of customers won't all pay the same price. They'll pay the right price—the smart price.

Endnotes

[1]"Is Cost Containment Impacting Pharmaceutical Innovation?" *Datamonitor* (September 3, 2008).

[2]Fulda, Thomas R., et al., *Handbook of Pharmaceutical Public Policy* (Informa Healthcare, 2007).

[3]"Opportunity Knocks for Big Pharma As Credit Crunch Takes Ever Stronger Hold" *Pharma Marketletter* (October13, 2008).

[4]Patterson, John, "Can Big Pharma Produce the Next Generation of Medicines?" *Pharmaceutical Technology* (August 8, 2008): 114.

[5]*Ibid.*

[6]Kollewe, Julia, "Drug Companies: Big Companies Besieged from All Sides," *The Guardian* (30 August 2008).

[7]Anderson, Pauline, "Clozapine Comes with Money-Back Offer," *The Medical Post* (May 16, 1995).

[8]Moran, Nuala, "UK Ponders Plan Promoting Payment Upon Performance," *BioWorld International* (June 6, 2007).

[9]*Ibid.*

[10]Thomas Nagle, The Monitor Group, "Money-Back Guarantee ... and Other Ways You Never Thought to Sell Drugs," *Pharmaceutical Executive* (April 2008).

[11]Interview with Stephen E. Gerard, TGaS Advisors, "The Future Is Now: Consultant's Spotlight," *Pharmaceutical Executive* (November 2007).

[12]Patterson.

[13]*Datamonitor.*

[14]Zhang, Jane, "Push to Compare Treatments Worries Drug, Device Makers," *Wall Street Journal* (April 14, 2009): http://online.wsj.com/article/SB123967153492015713.html.

[15]Thomas Nagle, The Monitor Group, "Money-Back Guarantee ... and Other Ways You Never Thought to Sell Drugs," *Pharmaceutical Executive* (April 2008).

[16]Prasad, Shishir and Rajawat, K Yatish, "TCS Takes the Lead in Result-Based Pricing," *Economic Times Mumbai* (September 28, 2006).

[17]Atchison, Duncan, "Big Changes in Outsourcing," *Computing* (June 26, 2008): http://www.computing.co.uk/computing/analysis/2219886/big-changes-outsourcing-4083077.

[18]Pinto, Jim, "Performance-Based Pricing," *Automation World* (May 2008): http://www.automationworld.com/columns-4163.

[19]Shapiro, Benson, "Performance-Based Pricing Is More Than Pricing," *Harvard Business School Working Knowledge* (February 25, 2002).

[20]Online advertising survey, PricewaterhouseCoopers and Interactive Advertising Bureau (March 2009): 14.

[21]"Badal, Jaclyne, "Consultant Lets Client Use 'Gut' to Set Final Fee," *Wall Street Journal* (August 21, 2006): B1.

[22]Nagle.

[23]Pinto.

[24]Inselbuch, Elihu, *Tort Reform: A Reassessment and Reality Check, 64 Law & Contemporary Problems, Contingent Fees, and Tort Reform: A Reassessment and Reality Check* (Spring/Summer 2001): 175.

[25]*Ibid.*

[26]Nagle.

[27]Shapiro.

[28]Lenzner, Robert, "The Vindication of Sumner Redstone," *Forbes* (June 15, 1998): 23.

[29]"Disney Sues Blockbuster Over Contract," *New York Times* (January 4, 2003).

[30]Gross, Daniel "The Dot-Firm's Dot Bomb: How a Leading West Coast Law Firm Killed Itself," *Slate* (January 31, 2003).

[31]Shapiro: 3.

[32]*Ibid.*

[33]Saul Levmore, "Commissions and Conflicts in Agency Arrangements: Lawyers, Real Estate Brokers, Underwriters, and Other Agents' Rewards," *Journal of Law and Economics* (University of Chicago, April 1993): 517.

10

Conclusion

"Pricing is the moment of truth—all of marketing comes to focus in the pricing decision."

E. Raymond Corey, *Industrial Marketing: Cases and Concepts* (Englewood Cliffs N.J.: Prentice Hall, 1962)

For a farmer, a year's labor is riding on what he does at the time of harvesting. For that reason, he rises earlier and retires later to pick up every grain. For a company, the revenues that sustain its existence all ride on harvesting the value it has created in the marketplace, and there is no other way to harvest that value except through its pricing. That is why Professor Corey had it exactly right in saying that "Pricing is the moment of the truth." Indeed, it is the moment of truth for everything a company does.

Yet companies continue to neglect pricing strategy, although today's pricing environment is far tougher than in Professor Corey's day. New technologies and globalization are changing the marketplace at a much faster pace than before and blurring the boundaries of many industries. Competition continues to grow in just about every industry, and the focus of that competition has been predominantly on price. Consumers have much more pricing information and are more sophisticated in how they use it. Now, on top of all this, the global financial crisis seems to have made carefree spending a thing of the past for many consumers. We are all value-shoppers now.

Perhaps it's a sense of helplessness that prevents more companies from treating their pricing more seriously. How can you bargain with a customer who knows your cost structure? What can you do when faced by a Chinese competitor who wants to undercut your price by 50%?

In fact, as challenging as this new pricing environment can be, the situation is not hopeless. We believe companies have gained more than they have lost. They can gather and process much more consumer information that enables them to understand their customers much better. They can personalize their product offerings and provide individualized customer experiences in ways they have never been able to do before. They have acquired much more flexibility in setting and adjusting their prices at a low cost; indeed, their customers seem to have become much more tolerant of price variations across demographics and over time, which gives companies unprecedented freedom in experimenting with different pricing mechanisms.

As this book has shown, all companies need to succeed is to use these new capabilities in a smart, innovative way.

Throughout this book, we have seen that many companies, small or big, high-tech or low-tech, have learned to use these capabilities to their advantage. Their experience suggests that the key to pricing in this environment can be summed up in three different lessons: about the value of customer focus, differentiated pricing, and smart pricing metrics.

Customer Focus

In pricing, as in everything else we do in marketing, the customer focus is imperative. To be smart about pricing, you have to know, first of all, what kind of customers you are dealing with. If its fans were not devoted and fair-minded to some significant degree, "pay as you wish" pricing would not have worked for Radiohead. If villagers in

Bangladesh were not as frugal and trustworthy as Muhammad Yunus knew them to be, micro-loans would not have been such an effective pricing mechanism and changed the lives of millions. If Syms had not understood how fashion-conscious and impatient its educated customers were, its automatic markdown pricing would not have been a smart pricing mechanism. If Priceline did not know what type of customers were price-sensitive when booking an airplane ticket or a hotel room, it would not have put in place the right screening mechanisms and attracted the right travel customers.

A customer focus also means you understand what customers value about your product or service. If you know what they value, then you know why; and if you know why, you know how to create more value for your customers and how to communicate with different segments of your target market about your product's value. Most important, you know how to price your product to capture a share of that value. Donald Trump recognized that what drives the value of a high-end apartment was not just the location and quality of an apartment unit, but the buyers' new neighbors. When he sold the condominiums in Trump Tower, he set the prices extraordinarily high in part to attract rich and famous buyers. Google recognized that the customer attention at the time of searching for a product and the click-through are what advertisers want, so it lets advertisers bid for keyword advertising. Big Pharma recognized that government agencies, insurance companies, and patients are all looking for efficacy in a drug, so some companies have begun to introduce performance-based pricing for pharmaceuticals.

Finally, the customer focus means paying close attention to customer buying behavior. Knowing how customers make their buying decisions, what and where they buy, and how much or how frequently they make purchases can point a company toward the pricing mechanism that can best secure a profitable, long-term relationship with its customers. Financial service companies pay close attention to customer profitability and the share of the purse. Manufacturing and consulting companies pay more attention to customer solutions. Food companies focus on the share of stomach. When this is done right, the product or service will be rooted in a strong customer desire, creating more opportunities for smart, innovative pricing. Amazon's Subscribe & Save program for recurring grocery purchases is a good example. By putting customers under a subscription plan for regularly recurring purchases, Amazon accommodates, rather than disrupts, customer buying behavior. We believe that there are many more opportunities like this in products such as diapers, cosmetics, women's or men's hygiene products, gasoline, fresh vegetables...many necessities we purchase on a regular basis.

Differentiated Pricing

One of the most enduring phenomena in pricing is that even for the same product or service, different customers are willing to pay different amounts. This is true for apparel, plane tickets, hotel rooms, restaurants, pharmaceuticals, software...you name it. For that reason, it is rarely a smart idea to set a single price. Such a price typically leaves too much money on the table or foregoes too many profitable sales, or both. The smart pricing manager should think of the old Chinese saying, "A cunning hare always has three burrows." Often, it's a good idea to keep three price points in mind when designing a well thought-out pricing structure: low, medium, and high. Such a pricing structure ensures that customers with different price sensitivities pay different prices so that a company can minimize the costly tradeoff between the money left on the table and foregone profits.

In the first years of the Internet, many believed that easier access to pricing information would destroy differentiated pricing. In fact, outside of a few categories, information technology has actually created more opportunities to charge different customers different prices. Throughout this book, we have seen many innovative ways to implement differentiated pricing, or price discrimination as economists bluntly put it. "Pay as you wish" pricing clearly allows fans with

different willingness-to-pay to pay different prices for music downloads. Syms' automatic markdown pricing creates a mechanism to
charge a higher price to those who care more about fashion and can
pay more, and a lower price to those who can wait for a good bargain.
Priceline's "name your own price" mechanism allows the company to
price-discriminate even among price-sensitive customers, who can
name different prices depending on their own personal and economic
circumstances. "Pay if it works" is also a good price discrimination
mechanism, as a drug or for that matter any product or service, may
perform differently for different customers. Indeed, it can be a price
discrimination mechanism in disguise in an industry where overt
price discrimination is ill-advised. Targeted pricing is perhaps the
ultimate tool for price discrimination, as companies use what they
know about different customers and target them with different prices
at an even more granular level.

Smart Pricing Metrics

Perhaps the most important lesson we have learned from the
many examples in this book is that no matter what product or service
you have to sell, you can use different pricing metrics to set your prices
in many different ways. Realizing that there is more than one way to
skin a cat or price a product can be quite liberating. For instance, the
publisher of this book might sell the book outright to a reader at a fixed
price. It could also "rent" the book out to readers for a fee or sell it by
the chapter. It could post the book online and charge a reader based
on the time spent reading the book. It could offer the book as part of a
subscription service whereby a reader could read the book and others
for free as long as the reader pays a monthly fee. It might even try "pay
as you wish" pricing or "name-your-own price." There are many possibilities, even for such a conventional product as a business book.

Of course, the choice of the pricing metrics will affect the publisher's revenue streams, types of readers, costs, and profitability. The

trick is to make the smart choice through careful research, and the smart choice is frequently the one that ties most closely with the value drivers for a product.

Innovative pricing is not for the timid. As many examples in this book suggest, companies' smart choices frequently entail breaking away from long-held industry conventions in pricing. The good news is that companies that succeed are rewarded for it. Radiohead has apparently been rewarded in many ways for bypassing all the intermediaries in the music industry and letting customers set the prices instead of imposing them on customers as the industry has traditionally done. Chinese companies break the taboo on price wars and take on competition using price wars as an effective marketing strategy to grab the market and to reorganize an industry. Time-sharing vacation houses and time-sharing corporate jets redefine the conventional concept of ownership and prices for fractional, time-specific, but not necessarily location-specific, ownership. Breaking away from industry pricing conventions in each of these examples is not only financially rewarding for many of the innovators, but also transforms the respective industries in some noticeable way. The bad news is that a bad pricing metric can destroy value, and more rapidly than almost any other single act.

Getting the pricing right is, in the end, both art and science. Like most business practices, the best pricing decision is grounded not only in theory, but experience and instinct. Ultimately, smart pricing demands not only deep customer knowledge and good economic intuition, but a healthy dose of street smarts. We hope that this book has helped you gain some understanding of all three dimensions.

INDEX